# FOUL DEEDS AND SUSPICIOUS
# DEATHS IN THE COTSWOLDS

# TRUE CRIME FROM WHARNCLIFFE

*Foul Deeds and Suspicious Deaths Series*

Barking, Dagenham & Chadwell Heath
Barnsley
Bath
Bedford
Birmingham
Black Country
Blackburn and Hyndburn
Bolton
Bradford
Brighton
Bristol
Cambridge
Carlisle
Chesterfield
Colchester
Coventry
Croydon
Derby
Dublin
Durham
Ealing
Folkestone and Dover
Grimsby
Guernsey
Guildford
Halifax
Hampstead, Holborn and St Pancras
Huddersfield
Hull

Leeds
Leicester
Lewisham and Deptford
Liverpool
London's East End
London's West End
Manchester
Mansfield
More Foul Deeds Birmingham
More Foul Deeds Chesterfield
More Foul Deeds Wakefield
Newcastle
Newport
Norfolk
Northampton
Nottingham
Oxfordshire
Pontefract and Castleford
Portsmouth
Rotherham
Scunthorpe
Southend-on-Sea
Staffordshire and The Potteries
Stratford and South Warwickshire
Tees
Warwickshire
Wigan
York

# OTHER TRUE CRIME BOOKS FROM WHARNCLIFFE

A-Z of Yorkshire Murder
Black Barnsley
Brighton Crime and Vice 1800-2000
Durham Executions
Essex Murders
Executions & Hangings in Newcastle
    and Morpeth
Norfolk Mayhem and Murder

Norwich Murders
Strangeways Hanged
The A-Z of London Murders
Unsolved Murders in Victorian and
    Edwardian London
Unsolved Norfolk Murders
Unsolved Yorkshire Murders
Yorkshire's Murderous Women

Please contact us via any of the methods below for more information or a catalogue.

## WHARNCLIFFE BOOKS

47 Church Street – Barnsley – South Yorkshire – S70 2AS
Tel: 01226 734555 – 734222 Fax: 01226 – 734438
E-mail: enquiries@pen-and-sword.co.uk
Website: www.wharncliffebooks.co.uk

# Foul Deeds & Suspicious Deaths in the
# COTSWOLDS

## NELL DARBY

First published in Great Britain in 2009 by
Wharncliffe Local History
*an imprint of*
Pen & Sword Books Ltd
47 Church Street
Barnsley
South Yorkshire
S70 2AS

ISBN 978 1 84563 074 4

A CIP catalogue record for this book is available from the British Library.

Typeset in 11/13pt Plantin by
Mac Style, Beverley, East Yorkshire

Printed and bound in the UK by
CPI

Pen & Sword Books Ltd incorporates the imprints of Pen & Sword
Aviation, Pen & Sword Maritime, Pen & Sword Military, Wharncliffe Local
History, Pen and Sword Select, Pen and Sword Military Classics and
Leo Cooper.

For a complete list of Pen & Sword titles please contact
PEN & SWORD BOOKS LIMITED
47 Church Street, Barnsley, South Yorkshire, S70 2AS, England
E-mail: enquiries@pen-and-sword.co.uk
Website: www.pen-and-sword.co.uk

# Contents

# Introduction

The Gloucestershire Cotswolds are full of picture postcard villages, thatched cottages and village greens. They look idyllic, and attract thousands of tourists every year. But every area has its dark heart. These pretty villages and towns have been the focus of all sorts of crimes in history – from murder to corruption, seduction to infanticide. This book sets out to show the uglier face of the Cotswolds, to explore the frustrations faced by villagers and how they reacted to the changing face of Britain during the eighteenth and nineteenth centuries.

Politics features strongly; Cotswolds' residents, it seems, have always been interested in politics at both a local and national level. Drink also features heavily – even small villages often had their own village pub, and this would be the centre of a community. After a hard day's work in the fields, many agricultural workers would end up in the pub for a convivial chat, a pipe and a drink ... but they frequently drank too much, and this could lead to trouble.

Of course, the Cotswolds straddle three main counties – Gloucestershire, Oxfordshire and Wiltshire – but Gloucestershire is at their heart, so I have focused on this area. Some of the stories from the Oxfordshire Cotswolds have been covered by Carl Boardman in his book in this series – I recommend that to those keen to look at stories from 'over the border'. I have also taken the liberty of including a tale from Cheltenham in here, although it is not strictly in the Cotswolds; but it provides an urban comparison to the largely rural stories here. Cirencester may be the main town of the Cotswolds, and it figures prominently in this book; but by no means can it be described as urban. The inclusion of Cheltenham offers the reader a better balance of stories.

Searching through the archives, I found many more fascinating Gloucestershire stories that would been ideal for this book. However, many stories come from the local press, who, in the eighteenth century, were more interested in the salacious details and not so much in where the story was actually located. So it is with regret that I can't include the story of Anne Williams, who in 1752 poisoned her husband with white mercury because she was in love with another man. Her husband survived long enough to point the finger at his wife, and after his death, she was burned at the stake in Gloucester. However, I can't determined whereabouts in Gloucestershire she was from, so she hasn't got her own chapter here – although I couldn't resist mentioning the story in passing in one of the chapters. Other events didn't interest the class-conscious press as much as they should have; so the murder of Abigail Biddle by tinker William Loveridge in Bourton-on-the-Water in 1829 only merited the briefest of mentions in the local paper, as it was seen as the result of an argument between rival gypsy factions, together with a short entry in the calendar of prisoners – not enough to base a chapter on, although the story shows how the traveller community has had a long history in the Cotswolds, and its own share of tragedy.

I would like to thank the various archives that have provided me with invaluable help and advice. Thanks are particularly due to The National Archives, National Maritime Museum, Gloucestershire Archives, Oxfordshire Studies, and Helen Hills at the Rare Book Department of Cambridge University Library.

I would finally like to thank John, Jake and Eva Darby for their patience in bearing with me whilst I disappeared off to the archives for days at a time – this book is for them.

# CHAPTER 1

# Nothing to Convict Them: The Murder of the Frenchman

## 1834

Francois Jacques Rens was a Frenchman who came to Stow-on-the-Wold to work and live a quiet English life. He ended up a victim of violence, robbed and murdered for his gold watch. He was also a victim of the economic misery, boredom and envy that permeated the lower echelons of Stow society in the nineteenth century.

Rens – his name anglicized by the locals to Francis James – was originally a businessman, a merchant working in the

*Market Square, Stow – Rens stayed at the* George Inn *here.* The author

Netherlands. After his business failed, he moved to England, working initially as a French teacher. He came to be acquainted with Mr Pole, of Wyck Hill House near Stow, who was a director of the Bank of England and treasurer of the Stow Provident Bank. Pole managed to secure Rens the position of actuary of the bank in around 1827, and Rens duly moved to Stow. He was, by all accounts, an upstanding member of his adopted community, teaching French to the local children in his spare time and being, in the words of the *Oxford Journal*, of 'agreeable manner'. He was seen as fulfilling his job at the bank with 'unprecedented integrity'.

He was also a creature of habit; many locals knew that after his evening meal in the *George Inn* in Market Square, Rens would go for a walk around town, often to the fishpool, returning to his lodgings with the Rogers family in Market Square in time for a cup of tea at 8.00 pm. Unfortunately, his regular habits meant that many people knew where they could find him and when.

On the night of his murder, Friday, 10 March 1834, for example, his landlord's daughter, Martha Rogers, had seen him leave for his walk at 7.30 pm. He had told her that he was only going for a short walk, and would be back soon. She knew that he usually drank tea at 8.00 pm, so would be back by then. At 7.45 pm, Rens was spotted walking down Back Lane by local carter Henry Sutton, who thought he was heading towards the fishpool. Rens was a large man, described as stout or fat by locals. He was an instantly recognizable figure.

Only minutes after Sutton spotted Rens, whilst he was near the fishpool, Rens was killed. He had been hit over the head, from behind. Initial reports stated that he had been struck with a 'blunt iron instrument'. Rens still had the old-fashioned habit of wearing a wig, and the force of the blow to his head had sent both his hat and wig falling to the ground. His gold watch and purse were both missing.

He was found shortly afterwards by carrier Samuel Harris, who had gone to feed his horses. As it was a winter's night, it was dark around Back Lane, and Harris had to use a lantern to make his way safely. He came across Rens lying on the ground, and immediately made his way back to the *George Inn* to raise the alarm, before returning to the spot with ostler Stephen Brookes and gamekeeper Charles Shepherd. They lifted up the semi-conscious figure and Harris immediately recognized him. The three men carried Rens up to his room at the *George Inn*, and the local surgeon, George Hayward, was called over to examine him. He later said that Rens had several wounds to his head, the largest one being over his right temple, and so deep that Hayward could see his skull. Rens survived for about four hours, in great agony, but finally died around midnight.

An Inspector Adamson was sent up from the London police to help the local authorities to find out what had happened. Many witnesses came forward to try and point the finger at various locals, and it was up to Adamson to sort out the witnesses' often conflicting statements, and to work out what might have happened.

It says something about society at that time that people seemed equally shocked by the theft of Rens' gold watch as they were by the murder. A reward of £200 was put up by a local wealthy man, John Darby Charles, for evidence received, but the reward posters focused on detailed descriptions of the watch, with the facts of the murder listed further below, almost as an afterthought.

From an early point in the police investigation, the focus was on two local men – John Clifford and Richard Cox. Clifford was a stonemason, and possibly also the owner of a beer shop. At this time, people often had more than one job to make an adequate living. He had been in possession of a hefty wooden stick the night of the murder, and his trousers were stained – with blood, the police believed. Cox was a sawyer, and the evidence against him was particularly flimsy, being largely that there were a few minutes when he had no alibi, and that he was also known to be a poacher (the police obviously saw poachers has having the potential for criminality towards men as well as animals).

Inspector Adamson searched Cox's house and found rabbit nets and night lines, and other poaching paraphernalia designed to catch pheasants – all of which, it was implied, was evidence that Cox may have been involved in Rens' murder.

# MURDER
### AND
# ROBBERY!!
# 200 POUNDS
# REWARD.

Whereas a barbarous **MURDER** was committed, on the Evening of the 10th of March, at *Stow-on-the-Wold*, on the Body of Mr. FRANCES JAMES RENS, of *Stow* aforesaid, and a

# *Gold Watch*

taken from his Person.

The **WATCH** is a double cased Repeater, capped, it strikes on a Bell inside the case, and can occasionally be made a dumb Repeater. it is of a large size, rather old fashioned, and of Foreign make, although there is the word *London* on the Dial. The Gold Chain is made of round Links, cut in a Diamond Pattern, and has been repaired. The Seals are of a plain make, Stirrup Pattern, and the impression on one is supposed to be a Stag.

This is to give Notice, that the above Reward will be paid by Mr. JOHN D. CHARLES, *Stow-on-the-Wold*, to any Person who shall give such information, as may lead to the conviction of the Perpetrator or Perpetrators of the said Murder.

*N.B. Should the above described Watch be offered for sale or in Pawn, to any Person, he is requested to detain the Offerer, and give immediate information to* Mr. J. D. CHARLES, *of Stow-on-the-Wold, Gloucestershire.*

*Stow-on-the-Wold, March* 11, 1834.

**N. B. The above Reward of 200 POUNDS, will be given, and his *Majesty's Pardon* granted to any Accomplice, who is not a Principal in the said Murder, and shall give such information concerning it as may lead to the conviction of the Murderer.**

Ho 44 / 27 / 180

R LANE, PRINTER, STOW.

*The wanted poster issued after Francois Rens' death.* The National Archives (ref HO 44-27 (180))

Cox had also been the owner of the wooden stick in Clifford's possession; he had sold it to a man named Smith the night of the murder. Cox claimed to have been given the stick originally by a chimney sweep, Mr Ruff, in return for a quart of beer. Cox had then sold the stick on whilst in Clifford's beer shop, and Clifford had then taken it from Smith, saying he would get the stick varnished for him.

Clifford said he then kept the stick in his possession, until Adamson retrieved it from him the following Wednesday. Adamson noted that when he took it, it was damp, as though it had just been washed, and was covered in scrapes, as though it had been used to strike something or someone. Clifford's clothes were then checked, and his trousers, which he admitted to have been wearing on the night of the murder (he probably did not have an extensive wardrobe, as he was still wearing the trousers when interviewed) had a stain on the right knee – possibly, Adamson thought, from blood.

Clifford and Cox were arrested within a week of the murder and held at Gloucester Gaol. There seemed to be little rationalizing about the men's motive; for example, Clifford shouldn't have needed to kill a man for money; he was a literate man with a trade, and seemed to have had a regular income and work. By the time of his arrest, he was twenty-nine years old, married with a toddler daughter, a respectable, hard-working family man. He was known in the town and would surely have been recognized – he was tall for the area at that time, being nearly six foot tall, and was scarred from smallpox. And although Richard Cox was illiterate, he too was in a trade and employed.

Luckily, even in those relatively unenlightened times, there was very soon doubt about their guilt. Even as they lay languishing in Gloucester Gaol, the *Oxford Journal* reported that there was a 'mystery' about who had killed Francois Rens. On 27 March, just over two weeks after the murder, it was reporting that the two men were still in custody, but that nothing had been found to convict them. The police commented that they thought the murderer was local – but implicit in this statement was the belief that although local, he may not have been either of the men arrested for the crime.

However, the two were charged with murder and their case was scheduled for the next Assizes. But justice eventually prevailed; it was decided that there was no case to answer for either man, and they were discharged.

Investigations continued for some time, and eventually, another potential perpetrator was identified. This time, it was Edwin Jeffrey, a twenty-one-year-old labourer working for a local farmer. He had aroused suspicions by trying to take an expensive gold watch to be mended at a local watch-mender's. The latter didn't believe Edwin's story about being given the watch by his brother, who was a servant, and voiced his suspicions to the police.

Semi-literate Jeffrey, condemned by the media for being short (although he was in fact two inches taller than Richard Cox) and having a squint, was not blessed with education or good looks, and probably only just made a living in Stow. He lived-in as Farmer Ellis's labourer but had to share a bed with Ellis's young apprentice, Lewis Hutchings. He didn't look like the sort of man who could own a gold watch. That was more the sort of thing that Francois Rens would have had ... could it have been the dead man's watch that Edwin had tried to mend?

Edwin Jeffrey didn't have the education to help himself. At the start of his trial, he attempted to plead guilty. The judge warned him that he was not doing himself any favours, and that he might as well wait for the jury to hear all the evidence. Jeffrey agreed and changed his plea to not guilty. However, he had already signed a confession (with a mark), stating that robbery had been his motivation for killing Rens, as he knew the Frenchman carried a gold watch with him. Although he had also taken Rens' purse, it had only contained eighteen pence, and was not the motive for the murder.

Jeffrey had frequently seen Rens out on his regular nightly walks, and spotted the watch hanging from his pocket. A poor man, with no hope of ever getting a well-paid job, he coveted the gleaming item, and planned to rob the Frenchman for it. He had watched Rens pass by on his evening walk on 10 March 1834, and followed him, having retrieved a stout stick from the nearby slaughterhouse. Jeffrey explained that he watched Rens go round the pool. He guessed what route he would take, and stood by the gate leading to a field owned by the rector, Richard Vavasour, until Rens came by. The Frenchman courteously wished Jeffrey goodnight and tried to pass him by. Jeffrey then struck him with the stick, causing Rens to cry out. Jeffrey claimed that he had only struck Rens once, but that the latter had hurt his head further when he fell to the ground.

Jeffrey immediately hid the watch he had retrieved from Rens' pocket in the garden of a nearby house. He was lucky not to get caught immediately, for he seems to have seen and been seen by several locals shortly afterwards. He saw Samuel Harris with his lantern walking down Back Lane; then he saw his colleague Lewis Hutchings in the nearby stables; and finally, he saw labourer William Richens in an alley, who told him something was the matter. With some cheek, or bravado, he then took a lantern and went back down to where the body was. Several people were already clustered around the body, placing it in a chair to carry Rens back to his lodgings. Jeffrey was one of the men who helped take it there.

Jeffrey admitted that he was now 'alarmed' and could not sleep all that night, after having discussed the affair with Lewis Hutchings, with whom he shared a bedroom (although he did not admit to Hutchings that he was the murderer). He waited three days before retrieving the hidden watch and hiding it in a new location. He hid it on a wall, covered in hay, for another month, although he checked on it regularly. After that, he couldn't resist wearing it, although he was careful to hide it in his hand when he wanted to check the time, and then put it carefully in his pocket.

On 10 September 1834, six months after the murder, he realized that it didn't work properly. Being poorly educated and not very bright, he seems to have imagined that people would have short memories in Stow – and promptly took the murdered man's watch to a local man, George Thornton, to be fixed. Thornton recognized it as a French watch, and felt it didn't suit Jeffrey. He offered him another watch in exchange, which Jeffrey agreed to. Two weeks later, a watchmaker, George Payne, saw the watch being held by Thornton, and recognized it as Rens'. He had often seen Rens wear it, on a brown watchguard. Jeffrey's desire for a nice gold watch that worked had finally led to his capture.

On 15 April 1835, Edwin Jeffrey was hanged in a public execution outside Gloucester Gaol. Newspapers reported large crowds gathering to witness his death – public executions were often great social events for people, with almost a holiday atmosphere prevailing. Jeffrey, poor, plain, and ill-educated, was not in a festive mood and was seen praying until the moment he dropped.

# CHAPTER 2

# Worked Enough to Kill a Horse: The Northleach Prison Inquiry

## 1842

On Monday, 10 October 1842, a sawyer named Charles Beale died at his father's house in Burton Street, Cheltenham, of tuberculosis. He was just twenty-three. His illness and subsequent death sparked an inquiry into the conditions at Northleach House of Correction that shook the Government and people across Victorian England.

Charles Beale had spent six months as a prisoner at Northleach. He went in healthy, but came out with badly diseased lungs – and with four other recently discharged prisoners, he complained about the treatment he had received whilst incarcerated. When he gave evidence to the inquiry, his final words were that if he died, it would be because he had been murdered by the treatment given to him in Northleach.

Charles Beale was born in 1818 in Cheltenham, the son of Nathaniel and Alice Beale. He was from a poor family. His father was a sawyer who doesn't seem to have been very successful. In 1841, Nathaniel and Alice were living with Nathaniel's elder brother Robert – also a sawyer – and were in later years both described as paupers. By 1871, widower Nathaniel was an inmate of the Charlton Kings Workhouse.

Illiterate Charles had set up work in Cheltenham as a sawyer, following in his family's tradition. He worked with a partner, Joseph Rowley, an older man, also from the town, whom he had known since about 1835. Times were hard and they needed materials to work with. On 19 February 1842, they stole two mahogany boards from Jeremiah Wheeler. They were unlucky men, though, and were charged with the theft

*Northleach House of Correction.* The author

three days later. They were given six months' imprisonment each, to be served at the Northleach House of Correction.

An inquiry into the conditions at Northleach House of Correction had been instigated initially after several applications for parish poor relief were made by people who claimed they were disabled, and unable to work, as a result of their treatment whilst previously inmates of the prison. These applications for help were becoming so frequent that two members of the Cheltenham Board of Guardians had their attention drawn to it, and, deciding that something needed to be done, they mentioned it to the rest of the Board.

One of the Cheltenham Union Guardians was gunmaker William Hollis. He was one of a committee of four appointed by the Board of Guardians to conduct the inquiry into the treatment of paupers at Northleach. The inquiry started on 22 September 1842, by which time, Charles Beale was already gravely ill. Charles had applied for parish relief from Hollis at the latter's house shortly before the start of the inquiry, and Hollis believed that he was so ill that he was barely able to stand, and in an advanced stage of consumption. When he

*Burton Street, Cheltenham – home of the Beale family.* The author

tried to give evidence at the union workhouse, he was so ill that he had to be sent home, and he was eventually questioned on another day from his father's home in Burton Street.

The complaints that had been made about the prison were not about ill-treatment towards individuals by the prison officers; but rather, that the regulations governing the treatment of prisoners at that time were such as would damage the prisoners' health. Complainants said that the labour they were made to do was excessive; that the quantity and quality of prison food was poor and that the cells were damp and unwholesome. In short, according to the press, men who entered the prison in good health, frequently left it malnourished, ill and unable to work.

Northleach House of Correction was opened in 1792 as a prison for up to thirty-seven petty offenders. It was designed to be an 'improved' model of prison, to replace the notoriously overcrowded and unsanitary earlier versions. Although designed for petty criminals, security was tight, with the cell blocks being positioned at the end of exercise yards which in turn radiated out from the prison keeper's house.

Four other men apart from Charles Beale had lodged complaints about their treatment in the prison. They were all working-class men, jailed for economic crimes caused through desperation.

The first man was Charles Beale's colleague Joseph Rowley. In 1842, he was about forty-one, married to Elizabeth and with two children – twelve-year-old George and ten-year-old Mary Ann. Prior to his conviction, he had been living with his family at Soho Place, Coach Road, Cheltenham. In 1842, Joseph had been fit, and had worked until the moment he had been arrested; but he was ill for most of his imprisonment. He blamed his illness on being overworked, not having enough to eat, and from being made to sit in a cold, damp cell whilst he was still sweaty from working on the treadmill. He told the inquiry that men were often so sweaty when they came off the treadmills that they could wring the sweat out of their shirts, and let it run on the ground.

The second man was illiterate labourer Joseph Wilson, aged forty-six. He had been found guilty of deserting his family in March 1841, and given two months' hard labour at Gloucester. Like many poor men, Wilson had left his family in order to go searching for work. His wife was aware of this and had sanctioned his absence; indeed, when she gave evidence to the inquiry, she objected to the crime he had been convicted, saying that he had not deserted his family, but had simply gone looking for work. She said that although he was strong and healthy, he was worried about his inability to give his family enough food.

So Joseph Wilson had left home to find work and therefore the money to ensure his family was well-fed; but in his absence his wife, Ann, was unable to support her family. She told the inquiry she had had seven children and that she and they had had to leave their home in London Road, Cheltenham, to be admitted to the Charlton Kings Workhouse. The Admission and Discharge Book for the workhouse shows that five of Joseph's children were in the workhouse at the start of 1841. The eldest daughter, Ann, was briefly discharged at the end of

January to go into service, but was readmitted on 4 March. Two weeks after her readmittance, on 15 March 1841, Joseph Wilson was formally convicted of desertion. His children remained in the workhouse until 10 May 1841, after a spell of over five months inside.

As a result of the Wilsons being admitted to the workhouse, the Cheltenham Poor Law Union Guardians instigated criminal proceedings under the 1824 Vagrancy Act as a husband's absence left the Poor Law Union to pay for the upkeep of his wife and children – and they wanted these costs back. During his absence from home, Wilson had found work elsewhere, and procured a house for his family, but he had been arrested two days before he had intended to return and collect his family. He was given a two months' prison sentence, and was so ill by the time he was released that he was no longer able to work. Wilson died shortly before Charles Beale. His three-year-old daughter Jemima died the same year; and his wife died shortly after giving evidence to the inquiry. Although his surviving daughters found work, his thirteen-year-old son Jesse was admitted to the workhouse several more times in 1842 and 1843, absconding at least twice, before finding a home with an aunt and uncle.

The list of inmates for Northleach, recorded on 28 June 1842, notes the presence of both Beale and Rowley – and also records another prisoner, John Newton, age forty, 'rogue and vagabond', who on 14 April that year had been sentenced to three months' hard labour for deserting his family. Newton, a shoemaker, was a widower with three young children, aged between three and seven. He told the inquiry that he had three young children in the workhouse, but because he was short of work, he had to leave them and seek work elsewhere. He was arrested in Gloucester, and charged with leaving his children chargeable to the parish of Cheltenham.

John Newton had gone into prison in good health, but, again like Wilson, was so ill after his release, on 7 July, that he was unable to go back to work. He told the inquiry that all the prisoners complained about how cold the cells were, and that several had fainted. They were put on the cold floor until they

*Charlton Kings Workhouse admission records for the Newton children.*
Gloucestershire Archives (ref G/CH/60/2)

regained consciousness – and then made to work on the wheel again.

As a result of his inability to work after leaving Northleach, John Newton had to again be admitted to the workhouse at Charlton Kings, and put on a special diet to aid his recovery. His readmittance to the workhouse also meant that his children had to stay there as well. The records show that the three children were admitted at least seven times between July 1841 and December 1842.

Wilson was sure that the prison regime had made him ill. He told the inquiry that he always came off the wheel sweating a lot, but then would be put straight into a cold cell, with nothing but a cold stone to sit on. As a result, he developed shivering colds that got worse and worse. By the end of his imprisonment, he was barely able to work.

Even the dreaded workhouse seems to have been preferable to prison in some respects, despite its bad reputation. John Newton told the inquiry that the food in Northleach House of Correction was so poor that it was inferior to the workhouse meals.

The final man was labourer John Cooke, a poor young man who had been found guilty of stealing from an orchard, and sentenced to six weeks' imprisonment. A pauper, he had probably been desperate for food, and so had taken what must have looked like appetizing pears. In rural areas at this time, there was considerable friction between landowners and the working-class. The landowners were keen to protect their land and the produce grown on it; the labourers and other working men of the neighbouring villages saw open land as theirs by tradition, history and right, and resented the gentry trying to stop them from taking produce, or hunting game, on these pieces of land. Courts, though, being more sympathetic to the landowners generally, invariably found against the poor in such cases. John Cooke was found guilty and sent to Northleach. He left the prison to be admitted to the workhouse, and had to be brought from there to the inquiry in a wheelchair, now unable to walk. He said that he had asked the doctor to let him get off the treadmill when he was ill, but the doctor wouldn't agree to this request. When he finally stopped to rest, the overseer threatened him, and he had to keep working, even though he was tired and prone to fainting.

John Cooke explained that treadmill work varied according to how many men there were to share the work. He said that sometimes he was on the wheel for ten minutes at a time with five minutes off in-between, but that depended on the number of men working on it. If there were fewer men, the ones present had to work more. Newton saw several faint, and then forced back on the wheel as soon as they had recovered.

Charles Beale, in his evidence, painted a vivid picture of daily life at Northleach. He said that he had been put on the treadmill the first day of his imprisonment, and within two-and-a-half months found that he was getting weak and ill. He said the combination of hard work, lack of food, and the cold cells were the main reason for his illness. He described being on the treadmill with only four other people, and therefore having to work pretty much all day. With the lack of food to sustain them, he said the work was enough to kill a horse.

Eventually unable to work at all, Charles complained to the doctor, who ordered half a pound of mutton for him to eat – but he couldn't eat any of it, as it was so bad. After that, he said, he was given no extra or different food. Instead, he was put into a cold cell with the cold stone seat, and kept there for around fourteen hours a day, before going up to another cell for the night, where he would sleep in a hard bed.

When he had got a little better, Charles was soon put to work again. Although he was not on the treadmill, the new alternative was little better. Charles was made to work in a damp cellar, sorting potatoes. He spent two days there, working from six o'clock in the morning until six at night.

The cellar where Charles had to pick potatoes was on a level with a canal that intersected the prison yards (although a county surveyor later disputed this, saying it was some five-and-a-half feet below the level of the prison). The canal had previously been criticized by an inspector for being 'green' and perhaps contributing to illnesses suffered by prisoners; and being on a level with this water, the cellar was bound to suffer from dampness. Joseph Rowley said that in rainy weather, the prison was so damp that water often ran down the walls. According to the *Cheltenham Examiner*, Charles Beale was so hungry whilst he picked potatoes that he resorted to eating some of them, raw. Eventually, he became so ill that he spent the last three weeks of his prison sentence in hospital, before being discharged on 31 August. He told his mother, Alice, that he could not describe the starvation he had undergone in prison.

After conducting a post-mortem on Charles' emaciated body, surgeon David Hartley, from Cheltenham Hospital, said that the tuberculosis in Charles' lungs had developed over at least two to three months.

The inquiry found that the prisoners were fed potatoes and bread at 2.00 pm, then made to work on the treadmill for four hours afterwards, then locked up in a cold, damp cell until morning – and then made to go on the treadmill again from 8.00 am until 10.00 am – before getting any more food. Eighteen hours between meals – and then only getting scant provisions – meant that the men at Northleach were working hard without little energy to keep them going. The state of the cells, and the lack of comfort, must also have meant that they got little sleep and therefore never got the chance to re-energize.

The inquiry became national news and aroused the indignation of many ordinary people – although some were incredulous, not being able to believe that such conditions could exist. Newspaper editors warned local magistrates about their duties – for they were responsible for the management of Northleach House of Correction – if charges of neglect of duty were brought against any of the prison staff as a result of the inquiry. It was felt that magistrates were sentencing minor offenders not to a short term in prison, but to a death sentence.

The press and public were particularly incensed about the fact that labourers struggling to make a living and maintain their families were put into the prison system in the first place. It was felt that if a man was doing his best to find work and thus keep his family out of the workhouse, he should not be punished by being sent to prison, where, of course, he could not provide for his family at all. The ruin to his health under the prison regime could also mean that some would not be able to work on leaving prison, either.

The subsequent report by the inspectors of prisons confirmed that the prison cells were damp and unhealthy, and that the diet in Northleach was not adequate either in terms of quantity or quality. However, there had been previous reports, dating back to 1836, which seemed to indicate potential problems at Northleach – but these had not been spotted or rectified before they got worse. It was felt that the Gloucestershire magistrates must have known about the problems at Northleach earlier, as the inspectors of prisons' reports were regularly sent to all gaols, and the Gaol Act had explicitly stated that all prisoners should have sufficient food. In addition, the experience of other gaols – recorded in other prison inspectors' reports – showed the dangers of combining a lack of food with hard labour and poor gaol conditions.

The Gloucestershire magistrates met at the quarter sessions in Gloucester on 18 October 1842, and discussed the conditions at the prison. Not surprisingly, they attacked the bad press coverage, and tried to say that Charles Beale had had good treatment from the prison and from surgeons. One of those magistrates present, a Reverend Witts, laughably argued that as some people had been committed many times, the prison must be quite good, or those offenders would not have returned to it so often.

However, sense prevailed, and it was decided at the sessions to glaze all the windows at Northleach, to make the building warmer, and to put two-inch thick wooden tops on the stone seats the prisoners were made to sit on. The magistrates also decided that surgeons should examine each prisoner when he was brought in, and record whether they were already diseased when they entered the prison.

But the coroner's jury decided that Charles' TB was either caused or made worse by his treatment in prison, and blamed the conduct of the governor, surgeon and under-turnkey of Northleach. As a result, a commission was promptly set up by the Secretary of State, the Right Hon Sir James Graham, consisting of two inspectors of prisons, a doctor and a barrister, to look into the conditions at Northleach, and thereafter the conditions at other Gloucestershire gaols. Their findings – which criticized the staff at Northleach for negligence – were duly sent to the quarter session in April 1843. The chair of the court of magistrates at Gloucester, Mr Purnell, decided that a committee should discuss whether houses of correction should now only be used to house those awaiting trial and those who had been sentenced to less than three months' hard labour – with those having longer sentences being sent to Gloucester Gaol. The committee would also prepare a code of laws for both the local houses of correction and Gloucester Gaol. It was also decided that the negligent surgeon at Northleach, who had failed to react quickly to Beale's failing health, should be admonished (four magistrates voted for him to be dismissed, but were out-voted); the governor should be told off, and the turnkey be dismissed as he was guilty of cruelty towards the prisoners. The prison diet was also finally changed, and it was decided that persons given solitary confinement would no longer be sent to a dark cell every fifth day, as they previously had been.

But these discussions and inquiries were too late for Charles Beale. He was buried on 17 October 1842, a week after his untimely death, with a large crowd of people coming to pay their respects. Charles' death had come to stand for everything that was wrong with the Victorian prison system, and had shaken a lot of people, both locally and further afield. Things, these people hoped, would never be the same again.

# CHAPTER 3

# Dying with a Lie in His Mouth: The Murder of Mrs Millington

## 1743

Human life could often be seen as cheap in the eighteenth century. In a time when mere petty offences such as theft could receive the same punishment as murder, there was little to stop desperate criminals from killing from sheer panic or out of a belief that, quite literally, they may as well be hung for a sheep as for a lamb.

So a man could embark on a small-scale crime, and if he thought he was going to get caught, and hanged, might do anything to try and extricate him from that situation, even if it meant committing a bigger crime, because he would get hanged for either offence.

There were many petty criminals, thieves particularly, amongst the labourers of eighteenth century Gloucestershire. Class divides meant resentment from some labourers towards the more affluent middle-classes, and they felt little remorse about robbing them, either in the street as pickpockets did, or in their homes. Some men worked alone; others formed gangs to commit thefts more efficiently. Many were willing to take risks that might put their own lives in danger, and that was part of the thrill.

In Cirencester in the mid-eighteenth century, Thomas Cambrey was one man who worked as part of a group, committing thefts on people's property and homes in the town. One man he worked with was John Curtis, a labourer; another was one Thomas Steptoe, who seems to have been a local man, aged around twenty-one. During the day, Thomas worked as a saltman, but at night, he went looking for valuables to steal. Both John and Thomas may have been from more rural areas originally; a Thomas Cambrey was born in Great Rissington in 1723, and it would be typical of the time and region for a nineteen-year-old lad to venture to the nearest large town to find his fortune, by whatever means.

Meanwhile, at Bowling Green House, just outside Cirencester, lived James Millington and his wife Anne. By the time their paths crossed with Thomas Cambrey and John Curtis, in 1743, they were approaching seventy years old, enjoying an affluent lifestyle in a rural area just outside Cirencester. They had been married for almost fifty years – a real achievement in that day and age – their children were grown-up, and they were proud grandparents.

As was frequently the case in the days before widely available contraception, Anne had spent most of her adult years either giving birth or childrearing. They seem to have had six surviving children – Esther, born around 1705; Anne in 1707, Jonathan in 1711, Thomas in 1714, James in 1717

*The Bowling Green area of Cirencester: little remains that the Millingtons would recognise.* The author

and lastly Joseph in 1719, by which time Anne Millington must have been in her mid 40s. But she and her husband had known sadness too; in an age with high mortality rates, she had lost several children. In 1702, her four-and-a-half-year-old daughter, Hester, had died; a son named Jonathan had died in 1706 aged seven; and their first daughter, Elizabeth, had died in 1710 aged fourteen. Two other sons, both named Thomas, may have died in 1703 and 1704.

But there had been happy times, too. Their daughter Esther had married Edward Iles, four years her senior, in Stratton, near Bowling Green, in 1726. They had had at least two children – one, a daughter, also named Esther, was born in 1731. A Thomas Millington, possibly James and Anne's son, had married in Cirencester in 1735.

The couple was approaching their twilight years, knowing that they had had a long and happy marriage, that their surviving children were settled locally with their families, and that they had the security of each other and their solid house in the Bowling Green area. They were happy spending quiet evenings together.

On the evening of 25 October 1743, between 6.00 and 7.00 pm, James and Anne were enjoying one of their peaceful evenings, sitting in front of the fire with their grown-up daughter Esther, and her two daughters. Esther's husband, Edward Iles, doesn't appear to have been present. Suddenly, the front door burst open, having been violently forced, and Thomas Cambrey, John Curtis, and Thomas Steptoe, entered. They found the Millingtons, and demanded money from them. James Millington, who must have been scared and desperate to protect his family, gave them what he had on them, but it wasn't as much as the three thieves wanted. They had no scruples. Despite James' wife, daughter and granddaughters being present, they beat James up, and when they had finished, turned on Anne. They pushed her up against a wall, where Thomas Cambrey stabbed her in the left breast with a knife. Whilst the horrified family rushed to her aid, the thieves then ransacked the house, stealing £23, a great coat belonging to James, a gun, and several bottles of alcohol. They then made their escape.

Poor Anne Millington managed to cling on for life for a little while, in an age where effective medical intervention was low, meaning the chances of surviving such an injury were equally poor. It is no surprise, then, that three days later, she finally died as a result of the stab wound Cambrey had given her. Cambrey was now wanted for murder, along with his accomplices.

The men were soon arrested. Cambrey managed to get several witnesses to state that he had been at Cricklade between 5.00 and 6.00 pm on the day of the burglary. Another two witnesses added that he had been at his own house, two miles from Cirencester, between 8.00 and 9.00 pm. However, two people gave King's evidence that they had seen him in Cirencester between 4.00 and 5.00 pm that afternoon, so could not, presumably, have been at Cricklade by the time he had stated.

John Curtis also tried to round up witnesses. His said that he had been at the *Three Cups* pub in Tetbury between 5.00 and 6.00 pm, but, again, two people gave King's evidence that Curtis had then turned up at *The Boot* public house, again in Tetbury, between 10.00 and 11.00 pm, wearing a light-coloured great coat that, it was hinted, was not his.

Unfortunately for Cambrey and Curtis, their accomplice, Thomas Steptoe, turned King's evidence, and said on oath that it had been these two men who had robbed the Millingtons with him, and who were responsible for Anne Millington's death. Anne's daughter, Esther, also gave evidence identifying the two men. On the basis of Steptoe's and Esther's oaths, Thomas Cambrey and John Curtis were formally charged at the start of November 1743 with the burglary and the murder of Anne Millington.

The two men were tried on 10 March 1744, and found guilty. They were both sentenced to death. But only Thomas Cambrey would receive the death sentence. By the time of their trial, John Curtis was seriously ill, and he died less than a day later, at 1.00 am on 11 March, in the condemned room at Gloucester Castle.

John Curtis's death left Thomas Cambrey depressed and physically ill. However, by 17 March, he was regarded by the

Thomas Cambrey and John Curtis, for breaking open the House of James Millington, (commonly call'd the Bowling Green-House) near Cirencester, and robbing the same of 23 l. in Money, a Great Coat, Gun, and several Bottles of Strong Liquors; and also for murdering the said Millington's Wife.—— The Prosecutor depos'd, that on the 25th of October last, between Six and Seven o'Clock at Night, as he, his Wife, his Daughter Iles, and her two Daughters, were sitting by the Fire, his Door was broke open with great Violence, and the Prisoners (with one Tho. Steptoe, whose Trial is for some Reasons deferr'd) came in and demanded his Money; but not receiving what they expected, they beat him in a barbarous Manner, and push'd his Wife up against a Wall, where the said Cambrey (being all the while assisted by Curtis) stabb'd the said Millington's Wife in her Left Breast with a Knife, of which Wound she languished three Days, and then dy'd; and that after this they robb'd the House of what other Money they could find, which, with the Great Coat, &c. they carry'd off.——

*The Gloucester Journal's report of the Anne Millington case. Gloucestershire Archives* (Gloucester Journal, 13/3/1744)

authorities as being much better, and his execution was accordingly arranged for the following Tuesday. The hanging would actually happen by Bowling Green House, the scene of the murder.

Cambrey continued to deny responsibility for the crimes he had been found guilty of, despite the evidence from the family. There was some sympathy for him from the authorities; as he had been so ill after John Curtis's death, the local under-sheriff decided that he would be taken in a coach to Cirencester to be hanged, the coach having already been organized to take two other criminals onto Tetbury to be executed. Cambrey would be dropped off (pardon the pun), in effect, in Cirencester, and then the coach would proceed to Tetbury.

Accordingly, the following week, Thomas Cambrey was taken to Cirencester. A great number of people turned up to watch the event. They must have included a great number of the Millingtons' friends and neighbours, wanting to see justice meted out. There is no record of whether the surviving

Millingtons watched the execution being carried out right by their house.

Cambrey continued to deny his guilt until the end, and caused animosity when he added that he had never met John Curtis until they were sent to jail together. Unfortunately, one of the spectators had seen Curtis and Cambrey drinking together on many an occasion, and asked loudly how Cambrey could die with a lie in his mouth. There was no time for Cambrey to think of a riposte. He was hanged, and afterwards hung in chains near the house where he stopped the life of the wife, mother and grandmother who had just been enjoying a quiet night in until three greedy men broke into her home.

# CHAPTER 4

# Paying Off the Innkeepers: Hanged in Chains

## 1767

Robert Jones was a careful planner. He would choose a man whom he thought looked affluent or who might be carrying a sum of money worth stealing, and then lie in wait for him along that man's usual route home. He was a confident thief, who saw nothing wrong with using force or violence to gain what he wanted. But when he tried to rob a neighbouring farmer, he went one step too far – and paid with his life.

The eighteenth and nineteenth century Cotswolds were home to many opportunistic thieves. In a rural district, there was a large divide between the 'haves' and the 'have nots', with the wealthy being targeted by certain members of the poorer classes who wanted what they had. Often, the motive for thieves was not jealousy or resentment; they had no bitterness with regard to the more affluent, but simply wanted some of their money for themselves, figuring that these wealthier members of society would not miss a small part of their money.

Robert Jones seems to have regarded anyone richer than himself as fair game, and had made a career of stealing from them. His last victim was Stephen Matthews, a farmer from Hinchwick, a small village between Bourton-on-the-Hill and Longborough, on the Bourton Downs. Hinchwick, at that time as now, was home to a farming community. There were, at that time, around one hundred residents, and the houses mainly consisted of the farmhouse and related buildings.

Stephen Matthews was a successful farmer, who was known in the local community to be very wealthy. He regularly

*Hinchwick village.* The author

attended Evesham market, where he sold his animals. On
Monday, 21 May 1767, he had been at the market, and had
received about £200 – a large sum. After his business was
finished, he got on his horse and started his ride back home –
a distance of nearly fifteen miles. As he was often at the
market, and would ride the same route to and from home to
Evesham, his habits would have been known to many people –
including Robert Jones.

The simplest route for Robert Jones to take, assuming the
lanes would have run along similar or the same lines as
today's roads, would be to take what is now the A44 from
Evesham until just outside Bourton-on-the-Hill, when he
would make his way along the narrow, dark track over the
Bourton Downs to the village. Even today, the road is
atmospheric, overhung by trees. In the eighteenth century, on
horseback, in the dark, it must have been decidedly spooky.
The Cotswolds had long had its share of highwaymen and
robbers, and anyone travelling along the dark, uneven tracks
of the area, particularly if they had large sums of money on

them, would have been on their guard. But perhaps Matthews was complacent, or knew the area so well that he thought he would be safe.

Robert Jones took advantage of Matthews' regular habits. Knowing his route, he decided to lie in wait for him somewhere along the road to Hinchwick. In the dark, he lay

*The road to Hinchwick today.* The author

down and hid in some grass along the roadside, clutching a plough paddle to him, and waited for the farmer to pass. He had to wait some time for Matthews to return, and was almost asleep when he heard the farmer's horse approach.

Stephen Matthews made the job a bit easier for Jones. As he approached his property, he felt the need to relieve himself, and so stopped his horse to urinate in the grass. Two different versions of the story then followed; the first was that Jones had lodged a stone against a gate that he knew Stephen would need to open. As Stephen struggled to open the gate, and was still mounted on his horse, Jones had struck him and knocked him off the horse. The other story, that was reported two months later, was that as Stephen put his foot in the stirrup to remount his horse after relieving himself, Jones ran up to him and hit him on the head as hard as he could with the wooden paddle. Stephen fell to the ground, but Jones continued to hit him as he lay prostrate, before robbing him of seventeen and a half guineas.

Whichever way it happened, one fact was undeniable – Jones had killed Stephen Matthews and left him dead on the ground. His body, which was not found until the next morning, had several injuries, suggesting both unnecessary violence on Jones' part, and some degree of premeditation. Matthews' head was very bruised, and the plough paddle had fractured his skull. There was also an injury to Stephen's throat that could have been caused by a knife.

In small communities, rumour mills are soon active, and that was certainly the case in the Bourton-on-the-Hill area. As soon as news of Stephen's murder spread, rumours about the likely culprit also started to circulate. Robert Jones had, since the death, paid off money he had owed with local innkeepers, for ale, and had also, rather stupidly, boasted that he did not need any money. The locals immediately voiced their suspicion that Jones was responsible for the murder of their neighbour.

Two days after the murder, on Wednesday, 23 May, Robert Jones was chased and apprehended by a Mr Wilks of Chipping Norton and Joseph Knight of Stow. Stephen Matthew's watch and the rest of the stolen money – most of it, for Jones had not had much of a chance to spend it since paying off his ale debts – were found on his person.

Robert Jones remained full of bravado despite being committed to Gloucester Castle. He insisted that he was innocent, and said the watch was a new one of his, that he had bought at Broadway. However, there was evidence that Stephen Matthews had received a new watch seal from Worcester two days earlier, and this was found on the watch when it was taken from Jones.

Jones was seen as an 'audacious' and badly-behaved prisoner, who had to be handcuffed and chained to the floor in prison. But the bravado soon faltered when, on 3 August, he was tried at the Gloucester Assizes, found guilty and sentenced to be executed. From that moment, he was seen to express penitence and contrition, not just for Stephen Matthews' murder, but also for the other crimes he admitted to committing in the past. However, he refused to admit to having murdered one Mr Wynniat, despite officials' belief that he was the killer in that case. This allegation may have related to Reginald Wynniat, a Justice of the Peace for Worcestershire and Gloucestershire. He had died, apparently of a violent fever, at Stanton in Gloucestershire on 17 April, 1762. However, Jones insisted that he was innocent of that crime and asked that this plea of innocence be published to the world. He did not, it seem, want to go down in posterity as a serial murderer.

During the eighteenth century, capital punishment was designed to be a deterrent to other would-be criminals. The gibbet, which was similar to a gallows, was designed to hang executed convicts, and would be put in a position where as many passers-by as possible would see it. A recent act, the 1752 Murder Act, had allowed judges to impose hanging in chains as a punishment for crimes such as murder, sheep-stealing and highway robbery. The latter two were seen not only as affronts to society but also as a threat to the economy, so were punished severely.

Although gibbets were often put next to public highways, in order to attract the most public attention, they would also be put, where possible, near the spot where the executed person had committed their crime. Hanging the body in chains, often by placing the hanged body in an iron cage, ensured that the corpse could stay in situ for some time, the decomposing flesh

*Caxton Gibbet, Cambridgeshire: did Robert Jones end up on a gibbet like this?* The author

held in place by the surrounding metalwork. The eighteenth century lawmakers wanted their dead criminals to serve a moral purpose to others for as long as possible. Never mind the smell of decay that would inevitably pollute the local air – or perhaps, that was seen as an added deterrent to others?

On 5 August 1767, Robert Jones was executed by hanging. On the next day, which was a Saturday, his body was transported to the spot in Bourton-on-the-Hill where he had lain in wait for Stephen Matthews and bludgeoned him to death, and hung in chains there, to act as an awful warning to other opportunistic thieves.

# CHAPTER 5

# 'Put All the Knives Out of His Reach': Killed in Front of Her Baby

# 1862

Victorians are traditionally seen as prudish, moralistic people, tut-tutting their way through life. But the Victorians who moralized were not the majority. Most of the people in rural society in Victorian England had distinctly modern ideas on how to live life, and there was little tut-tutting from neighbours or relatives of those who chose to live in an 'un-Victorian' way. So Sarah Moss, a Victorian woman, was not ostracized by friends or family, despite a somewhat lax attitude towards marriage and the opposite sex.

Sarah was a native of Rendcomb, four miles from Cirencester. Born around 1829, she had witnessed tragedy in her life; her mother, Elizabeth, had burnt to death in an accident in 1856, and she had been put out to service at a young age to support her aged father, Richard, her only immediate relation.

At one point, she was a servant to the Reverend Bloxsome at North Nibley. Whilst employed by him, she started a relationship with a young local farmer, and became pregnant. She had her baby, a daughter named Elizabeth Louisa Moss, in the autumn of 1859, when she was twenty-nine, and the farmer admitted paternity. He was ordered by the authorities to pay one shilling and sixpence towards the maintenance of the child. Despite the baby's illegitimacy, Sarah had Elizabeth Louisa baptized at St Peter's Church, Rendcomb on 13 November 1859. Sarah and the baby lived with Sarah's infirm father, who was seventy-six at the time of his granddaughter's birth.

*The baptism entry for Sarah Moss's illegitimate daughter at St Peter's, Rendcomb.*
Rev Charles Jefferson

The Moss home was a secluded cottage known as The Kennels, near the vicarage on Cheltenham Road in Rendcomb. Sarah shared a room with her daughter. One of their neighbours in the village was John Mealing, a labourer originally from Guiting, who lived with his wife Mary, from nearby Barnsley, and their children – William, Ann, Charles, Sarah Ann, James, Stephen, Emma and Richard, born between 1835 and 1854. The Mealings were poor but law-abiding and seen as respectable people by their neighbours; their sons were sent out to work as agricultural labourers as early as possible, with William certainly being established at work by the age of sixteen. By 1862, he was working for a Mr Southam at Marsden Farm as an agricultural labourer.

William, the eldest child, was a tall, thin, man. Somewhat ungainly because of his height and build, he also walked with a stooping gait that many working-class men of this time had, from years of heavy work in the fields and on farms. He was an independent man, and moved out of the family home to lodge with nearby residents. Space must also have been a problem for the Mealings with so many children, and they must have welcomed the extra space caused by William moving out. In early 1861, William was lodging with Joseph and Elizabeth Williams in Rendcomb; but by the autumn, he was lodging with the Mosses – and he and Sarah developed a relationship, hardly surprising given their close confines. They were soon sleeping together, and Sarah became pregnant in the new year.

But this time around, the relationship survived. William and Sarah became engaged, and the banns were put up at Rendcomb church. The wedding was due to happen in October 1862; Sarah was heavily pregnant, but the couple wanted to marry before she gave birth.

*St Peter's Church, Rendcomb: where Sarah Moss was due to wed. She ended up being buried here instead.* The author

Sarah took her impending marriage seriously. She saved £6 or £7 towards the cost, and asked the police superintendent at Cirencester, Edwin Riddiford, who already acted as an intermediary to receive and pass on the maintenance payments for Sarah's child from its father, to try and get the father to give her another £5.

William was not, though, the most stable of men. He had a history of 'pains' in his head, and on Thursday, 16 October, he saw his mother, and complained of these pains. His mother found that he was not making sense when he talked to her. She told him later that she understood his illness, as she too suffered from a nervous complaint. William had sought medical advice over a number of years for his problems, and his father remembered him having an 'attack in his head' when he was a young boy. At one point, too, William had worked with his father for a Mr Cooke at nearby Rapsgate – and John Mealing remembered that on more than one occasion, his son had had to lie down for half a day at a time, unable to work.

On Saturday, 18 October, Sarah and William argued, and William returned to his father's house, saying he would not leave there again. He stayed at his parents' until Thursday, 23 October. Sarah came to visit him every day except on the Wednesday. On the Thursday morning, William felt unwell, and complained about the pain in his head, telling his mother he was afraid the pain would drive him out of his mind. Mary Mealing, concerned, answered that she hoped not, and asked him to pray to God not to give him more pain than he was able to bear. Mary was worried about her son's mental health, but had great belief in the local doctors. William had previously seen local surgeons Richard Larke and David Ruck (William subscribed to a local 'club', and Dr Ruck was the club's doctor) and they had both believed his complaint to be 'nervous' – or mental rather than physical. Mary told William that next time he went to The Kennels, he should get his money, pay to see Dr Larke, and ask him what he could do to help.

At one point, when William was at The Kennels, Mary had been called for by another lodger at the Moss house, who had arrived at her house in the middle of the night to say that William was ill and that she should come with him to the Kennels. When she had arrived, she found that Dr Larke had already been, and that William, who was sitting in a chair by the fireplace, was seriously ill. Both Mary and Sarah were frightened by William's illness. Mary sat with him and held his hands, which were freezing cold; Sarah ended up staying up with him for two nights. Mary stayed over too. One night she slept by William's side in his and Sarah's room, whilst Sarah slept in the other bedroom. The next night, Sarah and Mary slept in the same room as William, but in another bed, keeping an eye on him.

At about 4.00 pm on Thursday, William had a cup of tea with his mother. He was again poorly, and said to Mary that his head was so bad, he thought it would drive him out of his mind. Mary said again that she hoped not; but she must have been worried as she tried to contact Dr Larke. As he wasn't at home, she waited for him at his house, and on his return told him that William was threatening to kill himself. In fact,

William had been praying to God at night that he might not harm himself or anyone else. Dr Larke, it seems, was unsure what to do with such cases, and promised to make up some medicine by 8.00 pm that night. He had previously diagnosed William as having a common cold when he had first sought his advice about his head some four or five years earlier – but later realized that he was suffering from a mental illness.

William stayed at his mother's until about 7.00 pm, when he suddenly got up and said that he wanted to go somewhere, although he didn't know where. His mother pleaded with him to go to bed, but William said that he wanted to go back to Sarah's. Mary accompanied him to the house, but when they reached it, he denied it was his home. Mary tried to reassure him. Then Sarah beckoned to him, and asked him to come in and have a cup of tea. He went in, and she poured him a cup. It was a cosy, domestic scene, with old Richard Moss sitting peacefully by the fireside. But when Sarah went to put her child to bed, Mary Mealing followed her upstairs, and warned her not to be alarmed, but William was not 'sensible', so Sarah should let him talk as he needed to, but put all the knives and other implements in the house out of his reach. Sarah answered that she was not afraid; after all, this was the man she loved and was about to marry. He was the man who was going to offer her, her toddler and her unborn child security and respectability. His mother had said that they were good friends, and that William had said before, when he was ill and thought that perhaps he was dying, that if anything happened to him, his parents should be kind to Sarah as he loved her. However, William later told his father that Sarah had been told by a local woman that he put on his mental illness in order to get out of marrying Sarah; and Sarah had come to him with her concerns.

When she came back downstairs, Mary announced that she was going to go home, although William tried to persuade her to stay. He then said that if Sarah would wet his head with cold water in the night, he would be all right. Sarah, who seems to have been a kind-hearted soul, said that she would do anything he wanted. Mary wished them a good night's sleep before she left, and the couple answered that they too hoped for that.

In the early hours of Friday, 24 October 1862, William Mealing turned up at the home of Timothy Tarrant, the local blacksmith, who also doubled as the parish constable. Timothy had known William all the latter's life – and was, in fact, also his godfather. William knocked at the door until Timothy's son was woken, and looked out of the window. William asked for Timothy, and young Master Tarrant went to wake his father. Timothy hurriedly put on some clothes and his stockings, lit a candle, and went to the door. William was fully dressed, with laced-up boots, but minus his usual hat and handkerchief. His shirt front and sleeves were covered in blood. William said he had come to Timothy's house ready for him to arrest him and hang him, as he had murdered Sarah at his lodgings.

Timothy, incredulous, pulled William into his house, and made him sit down. He then sent his son to get Mr and Mrs Mealing. Rendcomb being a small village, they soon arrived and stayed with William whilst Timothy rushed down to the Moss cottage. He carried a lantern with him to see his way along the dark street, and was able to enter the house through the unlocked front door. The house was in complete darkness, but he could hear a child crying upstairs.

By now, Timothy must have known that something was indeed amiss, and, noticing a light in a neighbour's house, went there in relief, and knocked on the door. Joseph Robins, the occupant, answered the door, and together, the two men returned to Richard Moss's house. They went upstairs to Sarah's room, en route seeing bloodstains on the stair bannisters and walls, and on entering the bedroom, found her lying on the bed, with her throat cut. The bedclothes were off, and Sarah was naked, Timothy later said, up to her shoulders.

The razor used to kill her was open, lying on the bed, in the place where William usually slept, and Timothy took it and put it in his pocket. It was a cheap shilling razor that William usually kept on a shelf. He then felt Sarah's body; it was not quite cold. Sarah's child, three-year-old Elizabeth, was in her little bed in the room, crying, looking on at her dead mother. The scene was particularly gory for the little girl; there was so much blood from Sarah's wound – which had almost decapitated her – that it was running through the bed, through the bedroom floor, and into the room below.

Timothy Tarrant, although he was pretty sure that Sarah was dead, decided that the doctor, Mr Larke, should be sent for. Another neighbour went to find him, and the doctor returned very shortly. He asked Timothy to take William into custody, but then changed his mind, and called the rector, Joseph Pitt, to ask for his opinion. But in the meantime, Mr and Mrs Mealing had taken their son back to their house, so Timothy then had to follow them there. Timothy then had the hard job to take his godson into custody, asking him first, politely, if he had any objection to having handcuffs put on him. William said he hadn't, and Timothy put them on. William said his head trouble had brought on the situation, and he was sorry about it. Then he got on his knees and prayed. His mother was so upset at William's behaviour that Timothy and Mr Mealing had to take William back to Timothy's house and kept him there until back-up arrived.

Back-up was requested from Cirencester, and soon the superintendent, together with a sergeant and two constables turned up. The superintendent, Mr Riddiford, went into the Moss home and found Sarah lying on her bed on her left side, arms crossed, her throat cut from ear to ear. There had been no struggle, and as her body looked calm, Riddiford deduced that she had been attacked suddenly, while she slept.

The murder weapon, a common shilling razor with a black handle, was found at the scene, bloodstained. Not found was Sarah Moss's purse, containing a variety of coins. The money had been stolen by William, who had given it to his mother. She later returned it to Riddiford.

Sarah's aged father was told about her murder, but he couldn't believe it. He kept insisting that she wasn't dead – she had only gone into labour. Nobody could make him comprehend the truth.

William was brought before the magistrates at Cirencester, and spent much of the hearing sitting with his head in his hands. He refused to put any questions to the witnesses who were called to give evidence – they included his eleven-year-old sister Emma, who apparently added little to the evidence

*The burial entry for Sarah Moss at St Peter's, Rendcomb.* Rev Charles Jefferson

of previous witnesses. In fact, William said he was unable to speak because his head hurt so badly, and that had been the cause of the murder. When he was formally committed to trial at the next assizes, on the charge of wilful murder, William said mournfully that he hoped to be dead before then.

Sarah was buried at Rendcomb on 27 October 1862, but William survived to be tried. His defence made a compelling case for William's insanity, stating that he wasn't responsible for his actions, and that his neighbours also felt that he wasn't responsible, even raising the money to hire his defence team. The police superintendent, Riddiford, was blunt in his opinion – apparently, when he took William into custody, he said he appeared to be 'off his head'. This opinion, although more subtly put, was echoed by surgeon Mr Rudd, who had examined William on 14 October and found him to be bordering on homicidal mania. Two more surgeons then gave evidence to the effect that William was not of sound mind as he was suffering from a religious monomania.

The jury took only moments to find William not guilty of murder on the ground of insanity. But guilty of manslaughter, William was condemned, perhaps, to something worse than the gallows. If he had been executed, his suffering would have been short and those 'pains' in his head would have stopped. But as it was, his wish to die was not granted – he was sent to Broadmoor Asylum for the Criminally Insane, and died there forty-six years later, in 1908.

# CHAPTER 6

# Politics Takes a Battering: The Abduction of the Voter

## 1859

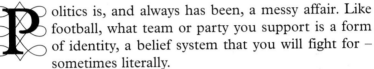

Politics is, and always has been, a messy affair. Like football, what team or party you support is a form of identity, a belief system that you will fight for – sometimes literally.

In the run-up to the 1859 election to appoint two MPs for the East Gloucestershire constituency, feelings were high. It was expected that the result would be close, and both Liberal and Tory voters were anxious for their party to win. It was a tense time; and the electorate was small. At this time, there was a property qualification meaning that only male landowners with land or houses worth at least forty shillings could vote. Although this amount had been the same since the 1400s, and therefore more people now met this criterion than when it had originally been laid down, less than a fifth of the male population were entitled to vote. So many party supporters wanted to make sure that those precious voters voted the 'right' way. The way in which they sought to influence the voters led to two high-profile trials after the election.

In the first case, three servants were charged with abducting one of Cirencester's voters in a bid to stop him voting Conservative. The scandal was that the evidence pointed towards the employer, wealthy Henry Pole of Stratton House near Cirencester, having made his staff carry out the abduction to his orders. At the subsequent trial, the judge implied that it was Pole who should have been the defendant and not his groom, groom's wife and gardener. But it was the loyal employees who were tried. Henry Pole escaped without charge, although perhaps his reputation suffered as a result.

The victim in this affair was the voter, one John Kibblewhite, who was born around 1800 in Cirencester. He was a road contractor, but a variety of tasks came under this job description, including drain mending and maintenance. It was not a well-paid job, and John's wife Charlotte helped the family finances by working as an upholsteress. If people had a problem with their drains, they would ask John to come and sort the problem out. John had often been called on to visit Stratton House, on the Gloucester Road in Stratton, just north of Cirencester, to fix their drain problems. Because of the frequency of this work, he had got to know the servants at the house – in particular, the head groom, Jermyn Coleburn, his wife Lavinia Susannah (known by her middle name), and the gardener, Walter Mullis.

Jermyn Coleburn, originally from Derbyshire, had worked in Leicestershire and London before moving to Gloucestershire in the early 1850s. His employer, Henry Pole,

*Stratton House, Cirencester.* The author

was also an incomer – he was a Hampshire fund holder, who had lived in a Wiltshire manor house, then moved to Warwickshire before becoming the squire of Stratton. He had a large house and a large staff working in it; besides the live-out staff such as Mullis and the Coleburns, he had numerous living-in servants, including a cook, lady's maid, housemaid and governess.

Henry Pole, as one of the area's gentry, would undoubtedly have been interested in politics, and wanted his own interests to be represented in parliament. He would be aware of how local people voted – elections at the time were open, with the secret ballot system only coming into effect in 1872. John Kibblewhite was listed on the register of electors as being on the right'; in other words, he voted Tory.

On the Thursday before the Cirencester election, John Kibblewhite spotted Henry Pole, with his gardener, Walter Mullis, passing by Mann's beer house – formally known as *The Plough* – in Stratton. He had heard a rumour that Mullis had been asking around for John, and so he walked up to him. Mullis said Mr Pole needed John to open a drain that had blocked. The following day was the nomination day for the election, and John wanted to get into Cirencester for an hour to hear the proceedings. But he also wanted to carry out the work for Mr Pole, so he got to Stratton House around 4.30 am, and did a full six hours' work before leaving for the nominations. He did manage to take a break, having two half pints of beer in the butler's pantry before he left.

After he had heard the proceedings in town, John stopped for a while in *The Plough*, although he didn't drink, as he felt he'd had enough beer that morning. By noon, John had returned, and immediately started work again. During the afternoon, about 5 pm, the butler invited him to the saddle room for a glass of beer. John was there drinking when Susannah Coleburn came in and asked John to have a pipe of tobacco, which he gladly did. She then asked if he wanted a cup of tea, and again, he said he would like one. Susannah told him to come with her, and so he accompanied her upstairs. Walter Mullis went too, but unlike John, he didn't have any tea. John took a cup, and drank it with enjoyment; but when he had a top-up, he didn't like it as much as it was very dark in colour. He asked Susannah to put some more sugar in it, and drank it. That was the last he knew, as he soon slipped into unconsciousness.

At around 8.30 pm, Henry Cozier, a young man who worked with Jermyn Coleburn in Henry Pole's stables, was asked by Coleburn to prepare the carriage, using Draper, one of Pole's horses, and then to run and open the gates to the house. Whilst he was getting the horse ready, Susannah Coleburn dashed out of the house with her bonnet and shawl on. Henry continued, opened the gates and saw the carriage out just before the supper bell rang at 9.00 pm. The carriage was driven by Jermyn, with Kibblewhite and Mullis in the back.

The next person to see the carriage was William Carpenter, who manned the Stratton turnpike gate. He saw the carriage through at 9 pm, and noticed Kibblewhite, whom he did not know, sitting in a leaning position, with a shawl over him. Carpenter waited for the carriage's return until midnight, when he finally went to bed. It was 1 am when he was woken to let the carriage back through.

Unfortunately, the carriage passed straight past John Kibblewhite's house, and his wife Charlotte spotted it. She noticed her husband sitting in the carriage, with his head lying on one side. She could not understand why her husband was not dropped off at home, and even more confused when he failed to turn up at all that night.

Shortly after 10.00 pm, David Cove, landlord of the *King's Head* in the village of Ashton Keynes, just over the Wiltshire border, was called on by an old colleague of his, Jermyn Coleburn. They had known each other for several years, when Jermyn had worked for a Colonel Shirley in the village, and lived at his house. With him was a man who, Jermyn explained, was a drunk whom he had picked up. Could Cove find him a bed? When Cove replied that he couldn't without turning someone out, Jermyn admitted to him that Henry Pole had asked for Kibblewhite to be sent to the *King's Head*. Cove should keep him concealed until 4.00 pm the next day, polling day, so that he could not vote. If Cove agreed to this, he would have Coleburn's eternal respect. Cove, quite reasonably, asked who the man was. Jermyn told him that it was a man called Kibblewhite, who was from Cirencester. At last, Cove gave in, mainly because he didn't think Kibblewhite was in any state to travel any further that night. Walter Mullis then brought John Kibblewhite in from the carriage, and took him up to bed. Susannah Coleburn then gave Cove's wife, Mary Ann, a bottle, about an inch long, containing a dark liquid. Mrs Cove noticed the label on it straightaway: 'Laudanum – poison'. Susannah told Mrs Cove to get a drop of rum in the morning, and put 20 drops of the liquid into it, presumably to keep John Kibblewhite quiet until after the election.

After they had put Kibblewhite to bed, the rest of the Stratton party stayed on for about half an hour, drinking beer and smoking tobacco. Eventually they left, and Cove went and sat up with the sick man until 1.00 am, as he was so worried about the state of Kibblewhite's health. Cove then visited Kibblewhite another four times between one and seven o'clock, because of the latter being sick.

In the morning, John Kibblewhite woke up in a strange bed, in a strange room – without the slightest idea of where he was or what he was doing there.

The Coves were already downstairs, having breakfast and chatting to one of their lodgers, a travelling draper from Gloucester named John Williamson. One of the subjects of conversation was the laudanum, which Mrs Cove showed to the draper, telling him how she had been instructed how many drops to give Kibblewhite.

While they were there, John Kibblewhite came down the stairs, and asked where he was. Cove told him he was in Ashton Keynes, whilst surveying his guest and being pleasantly surprised by the improvement in Kibblewhite's appearance. However, Cove still had to put on his gaiters for him, and lace his boots. Mrs Cove offered to make Kibblewhite a cup of tea, but he responded violently, refusing to have anything to drink. The Coves were united in their refusal to give Kibblewhite any of the dark liquid left by the Coleburns the night before. John Kibblewhite asked Cove to direct him to the Cirencester road, which he did, and then, at

8.00 am, he set off at a run for home. But before he went, he paid sixpence, all he had on him, towards his night's accommodation. John Kibblewhite was a scrupulously honest man.

John walked most of the way back to Cirencester, but when he got to Watermoor, near the hustings, he was picked up by a four-wheel carriage and driven to the hustings. His walk had made him feel very poorly again, and by the time he got to his destination, he found that he was not well enough to vote – or to do very much at all. He was taken to *The Bear Inn* and given some brandy and a cup of tea. At around 10.00 am, surgeon John Smith was called to examine Kibblewhite at the inn. He found him prostrate and immediately believed he had been drugged with a narcotic. The doctor believed he was not capable of voting at that time, and saw him to bed. He advised him to get some sleep, and thought that Kibblewhite was in shock from what had happened.

But John Kibblewhite knew where his duty lay. After a few hours sleep, he returned again to the hustings, and managed, against all the odds, to register his vote at the poll. John voted Tory, and two Tory MPs ended up being elected – Sir Christopher Codrington and Robert Stayner Holford. But at a national level, the Whigs triumphed, holding onto their majority.

The day after the election, Sunday, Jermyn Coleburn travelled on horseback to see David Cove. He asked him why he had let Kibblewhite leave his pub. Cove replied that he had never intended to keep him prisoner. Coleburn asked Cove how much money he wanted for the trouble he had been put to. Cove said Coleburn could give him whatever he liked. He was given fifteen shillings – a fairly sizable sum, given that the charge for Kibblewhite's lodging was just sixpence. Coleburn then asked what had happened to the bottle his wife had given Cove's wife; Cove said he would return it, and he had never seen such a thing in his house before, and didn't want to again. Coleburn was relieved, again implicating his employer – he said that his master, Mr Pole, would be pleased to see the bottle.

What is sad about this case is the fact that Henry Pole seems to have escaped prosecution mainly because of his wealth. At the committal hearing for the three servants, Mr Cripps, for the defence, admitted that the Coleburns and Mullis should be committed for trial but concentrated on convincing the Bench that Pole shouldn't be committed because of the 'slight grounds'. He argued that the evidence did not relate to Mr Pole, and that if he was committed for trial, he could end up with this serious charge hanging over him for months. He added that if he were committed, the news would have a negative impact on his position in life and society. Mr Cripps even suggested that Pole's wife Eliza might have told the servants to abduct Kibblewhite, without her husband's knowledge. He also said that Pole was not responsible for the acts of his servants when they acted illegally. Unsurprisingly, the Bench, which usually consisted of men from similar backgrounds to Pole, agreed that there was no case against him. However, when the others were committed for trial, and bail was set (£100 for each of the men; £20 for Susannah), Henry Pole was the surety for the bail. Did he have a guilty conscience?

At the trial, on 15 August 1859, Jermyn Coleburn, Lavinia Susannah Coleburn and Walter Mullis were charged under the Corrupt Practices Prevention Act of 1854 with the offence of undue influence in impeding and preventing John Kibblewhite by abduction and duress from exercising his franchise as a voter at the election of MPs in Cirencester. This was not the only charge of this nature being heard in Gloucester that day; one William Clarke was charged with using force, restraint and intimidation to prevent Admiral Charles Talbot from voting in the same election. Clarke was a voter, a Liberal, and wanted to stop the Tory Admiral from voting. Both parties' supporters were concerned that the result could go either way.

Susannah Coleburn was found not guilty halfway through the trial, as a Victorian male judge trial could not believe that she could have acted unless directed to do so by her husband, and so directed the jury to find her innocent. The defence, Mr Cripps, argued that the prosecution was acting as though Mr Pole was on trial, but the judge then stepped in to say he believed that those committed for trial were only 'subordinates', the implication being that they were working for Henry Pole. Throughout the trial, and that of William Clarke, it was implied that party politics were responsible for some of these legal actions, with party agents attempting to stir up events and people in order to gain publicity for their party. At the end of the day, the reputation both of politics and of Henry Pole had taken a battering.

# CHAPTER 7

# A Short-Tempered Boy: Getting Away With Murder

## 1851

John Hambidge had not had an auspicious start to life, being born the illegitimate son of a middle-aged farmer in Icomb, near Stow-on-the-Wold. One might have expected him to have had a struggle in life – but his struggle was not to do with his birth.

John's natural father, George Hambidge, was a wealthy bachelor, and highly respected by the villagers of Icomb. Having never been married, and getting on in life by the time John was born, he acknowledged John as his only child, and seems to have lived with his son since the latter was young. John was, like his father, seen as well to do – a good reputation by association.

The Hambidges were an old Icomb family. George lived there near his younger brother, William, also a farmer. William had at least six children – two were listed as 'dumb' in the census – ensuring the continuance of the Hambidge name in the Icomb area. Icomb itself was a village small enough for everyone to know everyone else. In 1851, the population was 140, the majority of whom were engaged in agricultural professions.

John was born in Icomb around 1826, by which time, his father was already forty-nine-years-old. Little was known about John's mother, apart from her name – Hannah Freeman. John's own name was flexible as a result of his illegitimacy; on his marriage certificate, he is John Hambidge Freeman, but his death certificate lists him as John Freeman Hambidge. His father referred to him as 'John Freeman otherwise Hambidge'. But in the nineteenth century Cotswolds, illegitimacy was

*Icomb village.* The author

common, and John's base birth does not seem to have led to any stigma or isolation amongst his neighbours as a result.

John was a striking man, tall at over five feet eleven. He had brown hair and grey, deep set eyes, with prominent features. It is no wonder that he found a bride early – for at the age of twenty, in 1846, he married Mary Ann Campion, a year his senior. They settled in Oddington, where Mary Ann had been born and raised. But by 1849, they had moved in with George Hambidge in Icomb. George was, by now, seventy-two, and growing infirm. Originally the owner of a farm of over 100 acres, he was now unable to manage the running of it, and had rented it out to Perrin Sturch, who now lived on the farm with his large family. George now lived some thirty or forty yards away. By 1844, he had had to employ a housekeeper, Hannah Eaton, but five years later, it was obvious that he needed his small family nearer him – so John and Mary Ann returned to John's old home.

On 15 October 1850, George Hambidge made an appointment for his solicitor, Mr Brookes of Stow-on-the-

Wold, to visit him. Mr Brookes was accompanied by his clerk, William Cornbill. In the presence of John and Mary Ann, the other men finalised George's will. Mr Brookes read over the finished will, and left it for a moment with George. When he went to retrieve the will, Mary Ann had it. It was still open; Mr Brookes did not seal it until just before he left the Hambidge house. In it, George had left instructions for the majority of his estate to be passed to John and his children.

*George Hambidge's will.* The National Archives (ref PROB 11-2153)

William Cornbill said that he had talked about the will twice with John Hambidge. The first conversation was in May 1851, at the *Talbot Inn* in Stow, when John had asked William if George had given any instructions to have the will altered. William, who had been putting up a horse at the inn at the time, answered that he didn't know – but perhaps Mr Brookes had received instructions. In July 1851, William saw John in the street; and the latter stopped to again ask if instructions had been received for the will to be changed. William said again that he didn't know.

George had not, in fact, changed his will – John's fears were unfounded. The will that was proved in May 1852 was the one written on 15 October 1850 – signed by George and his witnesses, Brookes and Cornbill.

In 1851, Mary Ann was pregnant with her son Thomas, who would be born early in 1852. George, retired from farming now that Perrin Sturch – himself no youngster at fifty-four – had taken over, was enjoying life as a landed proprietor – or so he should have been. But he was hiding something – something that must have prevented him from enjoying himself as much as a wealthy retired man should have been.

For John Hambidge was a violent bully, unable to control his temper, and, according to several witnesses, not averse to treating his father badly. George was a loving father, who had given much to his son – but this was irrelevant to John when he was in a bad mood.

From his childhood, John had been known as a short-tempered boy, who was unable to control his temper. It led him into a state of fury, and when he got older, people found that when he drank, he lost control of himself and became violent towards his father. When others tried to protect his father from his fits of temper, he would then turn on them. Neighbours reported violent acts by John dating back to at least 1843, when he was still in his teens. They said that the only peace George had had from this violent behaviour was the three short years when John had been living with Mary Ann in Oddington. George had become so alarmed at his son's behaviour after John's return to his home that he had called for Mr Brookes, his solicitor, sometime in 1851, to ask him how to protect himself from his son's violence. Mr Brookes had advised him to seek legal protection, but George declined this option.

George's housekeeper, Hannah Eaton, had also witnessed John's behaviour towards his father. She said that John frequently used to ask George for money. This is not altogether surprising; in the 1841 census, despite being of working age, John was not listed as working; and in November 1851 he was listed as having no trade or employment, and being unable to read or write well (unlike his father, who had a good hand). Perhaps he was complacent, given his father's status as a farmer and landowner, and believed that he should not have to work for a living. George obviously thought otherwise, and would occasionally refuse John's requests. When this happened, John would often resort to violence – perhaps knocking his father's head against a chair, or pulling him out of his chair and knocking his head against the kitchen's hard stone floor. On several occasions, Hannah had witnessed John threatening to blow his father's brains out. The last time he had said it, he had a gun in his hand.

On Saturday, 1 November 1851, the auspices weren't good. At about 10.00 am, a labourer named Giles walked past George Hambidge's house, and heard the raised voice of John Hambidge coming from upstairs. John called his father a rascal, and told him to go away. He added that his wife was pregnant and he didn't care for any of the Hambidge family. Giles thought it best to keep out of this family argument, and carried on his way.

At about midday, John went to the home of Mrs Watt at Icomb, near his father's farm, and asked her thirteen-year-old daughter to keep house for George that evening, as John and George were going out to Bourton-on-the-Water. Elizabeth Watt thought that John was quite tipsy; but she nevertheless left with him to go to George's house. They found a quiet domestic scene – old George sitting by the fire, and Mary Ann and her child sitting with him. John took a gun off the kitchen table, and Mary Ann asked what he was doing with it. John replied that he was going to take it to Bourton. Elizabeth Watt went upstairs with Mary Ann and the baby to help dress them, and John stayed downstairs with his father. By this time it was 1.00 pm. Mrs Watts and Mary Ann had only been upstairs for about ten minutes, when they heard a gunshot from the kitchen.

Mary Ann ran downstairs, alarmed, and found George leaning back in his chair, clearly dying, a gunshot through his heart. John was standing by him, with a gun in his hand. Mary Ann screamed, and Mrs Watts ran downstairs. By the time she got to the kitchen, John was supporting George in the chair, and blood was flooding the room.

At 1.30 pm, John came out of the back door and saw John Mason, a local labourer, who was walking down the road. John shouted out that he had shot his father – but Mason saw that he had been drinking, and so took no notice, continuing along the road. Mary Ann then came out of the house, at which point John called out to another passer-by, Eliza Sandells, saying he had killed his father. Eliza took more notice than John Mason had, going into the house with Mary Ann and finding the dead body of George Hambidge reclining in his usual chair.

Despite the neighbours' belief that John had been drinking, they agreed that he was in a good enough state to know what he was doing. John kept saying that he had shot his father, and then added that he had tried to fire the gun twice before, but it only went off the third time he tried.

Eliza rushed out to fetch a policeman, and was gone about fifteen minutes. When she returned, she found Mary Ann on the floor in a fit. She was unconscious for quite a time, her behaviour being a marked contrast to that of John, who was, apparently, quite cool and collected. He turned to Eliza and told her that he had killed George, and would be tried for his life. She was frightened, and became even more so when he went upstairs, and she heard him laugh above her.

At around 2.00 pm, the parish constable for Icomb, John Lane, arrived. Both John and Mary Ann were lying on the bed upstairs – Mary Ann still unconscious. The constable handcuffed John, but the latter then took him into the next door closet and took a paper out. John Lane, noticing it was sealed, put it back again. He thought later that it must have been George Hambidge's will. They waited for the Stow-on-the-Wold constable to arrive. John turned to Mary Ann, by now conscious, and told her not to worry, as the deed had been done and couldn't be helped. The fact that the gun had twice not fired obviously bothered him, as he went through what had happened again. He said he had dropped the gun on the floor when it did finally go off. He made various excuses as to how it happened; at one point he said it was an accident, and then that his finger had slipped. Could his finger have slipped three times, though?

He was also still drunk. John Lane said that he tried to sing a few times, and laughed, and asked for the sealed paper that he had tried to get out of the closet. He told Lane not to break the seal, saying it would be the worst thing he would ever do. John then charged Lane with keeping the paper.

Local surgeon Mr Jenkins arrived to examine the body, and found a gunshot wound in the upper chest, fired from within one foot away. The bullet had perforated the windpipe and fractured two ribs. The force of the bullet led a piece of George's flesh to become attached to the wall behind the chair where he was sitting. The gun had been fired at close range, and the bullet had passed through the body and out the back.

Despite all the evidence of his violent attitude to his father, and his knowledge that he was the main beneficiary of his father's will, the jury at his trial on 27 March 1852 inexplicably found him guilty only of manslaughter, after only one hour's deliberation. The insanity plea that the papers had confidently predicted would be lodged does not seem to have been. The prosecution had alleged that the evidence suggested the gun had been fired by accident; and the judge said that it had not been proved that John had been violent towards his father 'up to the very time of this unfortunate transaction'! But despite this, even the judge seemed taken aback at the jury's verdict, saying that they had been merciful, and that he wouldn't have been surprised if John had been found guilty of murder.

John received the trivial punishment of solitary confinement in the Gloucester Gaol for fourteen days. He was seen as being well behaved in prison, and so on 9 April 1852, he was set free, and returned home to Icomb.

Had the murder and his subsequent spell in prison changed John Hambidge? Perhaps. As the judge at his trial had said, before imploring John to take the opportunity to review and abandon the career he had pursued – in other words, his violence and drinking. He was told that the blood on his hands could never be washed away.

For the first time in his life, he now began to work. Unlike his father, he never became a farmer or landowner, working lower down the chain as an agricultural labourer, or day labourer. The trustees of his father's estate may have kept a tight ship and refused to have let their old friend's killer live a life of luxury. Or perhaps this was the penance that John made himself pay. Mary Ann remained by his side – although she would have had little choice in that day and age – and gave him several more children. She lived until 1891; John outlived her by four years, dying at the respectable age of seventy in 1895, his father's death a distant memory.

# CHAPTER 8

# Seeking to Inflame Communities: The Cotswold Swing Riots

# 1830

The industrial revolution was not greeted with unalloyed joy in the Cotswolds in the early decades of the nineteenth century. At a time when there was an agricultural depression in Britain, with low wages, not enough jobs to go round, and high prices, many poor agricultural workers were concerned about the introduction of new pieces of agricultural machinery that either reduced the numbers of labourers needed on farms, or replaced them altogether. The poverty facing many labourers was not alleviated by the pitiful amounts of money they could get from the parish. In addition, parish residents had to pay the Church Tithe, a cash payment to the local parson that contributed to his wages, and this was often more than the working classes could afford.

As a result of these concerns, many labourers started revolting, first in Kent, and then across the country. They burnt hayricks, smashed up machinery – in particular, threshing machines – and would attack buildings. The protests were nicknamed the Swing Riots, after threatening letters were sent to farmers and others, signed by a 'Captain Swing'. If the threats were not listened to, labourers and other locals would gather in intimidating groups to threaten landowners in person. Although Gloucestershire only saw a limited number of riots, they were centred on the rural area of the Cotswolds, and saw destruction and fear spread across the region in the winter of 1830.

The first trouble in Gloucestershire occurred on 26 November 1830, when a threshing machine, which was being

*Tetbury: scene of some of the rioting.* The author

transported to Tetbury from Wiltshire, was destroyed when it reached Newnton. The men who had destroyed it then travelled onto Tetbury and its environs, breaking more machines over four days.

Although the main rioting occurred over a short period of time in November, there continued to be isolated episodes of trouble. On the evening of Wednesday, 14 December 1830, for example, a fire broke out at the house of widow Mrs Pacey at Pardon Hill, three-and-a-half miles from Winchcombe. It transpired that the fire had been started at a barley rick, which had been destroyed, although others were saved by covering them with items from the house, such as carpets and blankets, which had been soaked in water. People as far away as Cheltenham soon heard about the fire, and became panicky, knowing what it probably meant. The rioters who had been breaking machines across the county had been at work again.

As a result of the crimes committed in Gloucestershire, some sixty men were held in Gloucester Gaol, charged with rioting and breaking machines in Northleach, Lechlade and

Tetbury. Most of the offences related to the destruction of agricultural machinery, the penalty for which was seven years' transportation.

Many assumed that there would be a special commission that would look into these cases as a whole, as similar commissions had been set up in other counties; but instead, it was decided to hear the cases at the Quarter Sessions, which took place in January 1831.

The media was happy to take a firm line with these rioters, regarding them as having disgraced their districts. As a result of the disturbances, the authorities sought to strengthen law and order across the county in the run-up to the Quarter Sessions. More policemen were recruited, with militiamen and pensioners persuaded to act as special constables. All the additional staff was seen as unnecessary, for the accused men were seen as sensible men who were aware of the illegality of their actions, and who were unlikely to stray again. They were mostly agricultural labourers, unsurprisingly, although there were some from other jobs. It was noted that the Gloucestershire men had not taken part in the more aggressive offences that those in other parts of Britain had carried out.

As many people would be looking at the Quarter Sessions to see how these political actions would be punished, a full bench of magistrates was present, among them such local bigwigs as the Duke of Beaufort, Marquis of Worcester and the Earl Bathurst. A Grand Jury was sworn in, chaired by the Reverend Dr Cooke. He stated that the jury had been called to carry out a serious and important duty, and that the country was looking to them to stop the violent protests that had been occurring.

Yet even as the Quarter Sessions began, meetings were being held in Gloucestershire, Yorkshire, Somerset and Wiltshire to discuss more destruction of looms and other machinery. The Gloucestershire Quarter Sessions were unlikely to stop the protests, and many men would be prepared to face the death penalty rather than give up their fight.

It was made clear at the Quarter Sessions that it wasn't just those who had physically destroyed machinery who should be punished. Anyone who had incited a man to commit such a crime should be found equally guilty. Although the economic reasons behind such actions, such as the price of wheat, were mentioned as mitigating factors, the jury's chairman then added that bad men would also encourage disharmony by seeking to inflame communities and mislead them. As was often the case, the education of the working classes was also held up for criticism; Reverend Cooke pointed out that reading and writing had been taught to people, but morality had not been.

The main case at the assizes regarded the destruction of a threshing machine, worth some £50, the property of Jacob Hayward of Beverston, near Tetbury, on 26 November 1830. Twenty-three men and one woman were charged with this offence – Thomas Bishop, Henry Compton, Samuel Seal, John Stancombe, Robert Ball, William Bigland, Joseph White, John White, James White, John Williams, William Cox, William King, John Cypher, Worthy Mann, George Wood, John Radford, Jeremiah Fry, John Woodman, John Poole, John Elliott, William Golding, Daniel Ford, Richard Ferrelee and Elizabeth Parker. All but two were local labourers (the exceptions being John Stancombe, who was a pargeter, and Jeremiah Fry, a baker).

Nathaniel Chapple, a special constable at Tetbury, whose main job was as a carpenter, gave evidence at the trial. He said that on 26 November, he was told by his superiors to walk down the Beverston road. At between 11.00 am and midday, he saw over 100 people standing across the road, with four magistrates watching them. The crowd was armed with weapons, including pickaxes, sticks and stone hammers, and some appeared to have been drinking. The magistrates tried to reason with the crowd, asking them to go home peacefully, but the crowd refused, saying that they wanted higher wages. Three of the magistrates promised that this would be done, although reports on the riots found that many of those in authority across the country later reneged on these promises. The crowd obviously feared this, and insisted that they would head on to Beverston and break the thrashing machines. En masse, they moved off. They made their way to Farmer Hayward's yard, and started breaking a threshing machine, reducing it to pieces with their hammers and sticks. Jacob Hayward, when he gave evidence at the trial, swore that the crowd had in fact numbered 200.

Nathaniel Chapple, who had followed them, but could not stop them given their numbers, saw Thomas Bishop, Henry Compton, Samuel Seal, John Radford, John Woodman, James White, Joseph White, Worthy Mann, William Bigland and George Wood amongst the men. Some of them were breaking the machine, and others, such as John Cypher, were either helping them or removing the broken pieces. Nathaniel spotted Worthy Mann breaking the machine with a large stick, together with Henry Compton, the two Whites, Samuel Seal and Thomas Bishop. Jacob Hayward believed Thomas Bishop to be the ringleader. He had asked Bishop what he wanted, and tried to persuade the men to go away, but they refused. His nephew, Isaac, added that it had been Bishop who incited the other men, encouraging them to break the machine.

After the machine was broken, the men went to another yard, broke into a shed and destroyed a horse-rake and a hay-making machine. Nathaniel seems to have left at this point, but between 5.00 and 6.00 pm, he saw them, still armed, turn up at the *Trouble House* pub. The first to arrive were Thomas and Samuel, who ordered beer, bread and cheese – their activities had worked up an appetite. On being told that soldiers had arrived, as back-up for the poor parish constables, one man said that the protesters would not hurt them. Shortly afterwards, whilst drinking in a room in the back of the *Trouble House*, the men were apprehended by the soldiers.

Another case that was heard at the Assizes involved another group of men, this time from the Fairford parish. Labourers Isaac Boulton, Christopher Ponting, John Mitchell, Robert Cowley, Charles Ferris, Edward Keylock, William Jones, John Lewis, Richard Adams, Charles Harvey and Thomas Mitchell were charged with destroying a threshing machine belonging to Fairford machine maker John Savory, also on 26 November 1830.

John Savory stated that at about 9.00 am on the morning of 26 November, a mob of around 100 men turned up at his house, armed with sledges, hammers and bludgeons. Mr

Savory, who must have been quite a brave man, gathered ten of his friends and relatives, including his brother Abraham and son Elijah, and accosted the mob, armed with sticks, stating that he was going to defend his property. The mob retorted that they would break Savory's machines, to which one of his men retorted that they would fight for it. The mob then rushed forwards, striking some of Savory's men. John Savory noticed Isaac Boulton amongst the mob, although he wasn't armed. Despite this, he managed to grasp one of Savory's friends by the arms, preventing the latter from resisting. Savory also noticed Thomas and John Mitchell, Cowley, Ferris, Keylock, and Jones, all armed with sticks. They began to break whatever they could find outside the house, whilst John and Abraham Savory tried to fasten the doors. The mob then proceeded to break down the door by striking a sledge at it, and rushed into Savory's shop, where they started breaking its contents with hammers. They went from there to the foundry, again breaking whatever they came across. When Savory eventually ventured out of his house, he found all his machinery, including a threshing machine, completely destroyed.

The accused men seem to have particular roles within the mob. Isaac Boulton was the ringleader, and gave the order for the machines to be broken, whereas Christopher Ponting arranged all the machinery in one place to be destroyed. Harvey and Lewis both had sledges to break the machinery, and Keylock and Adams had sticks to move broken machinery out of the way. But despite their actions, they were commended in court for having had good characters previously. Therefore, despite all being found guilty, the jury and John Savory asked that mercy should be given to them.

But one of the men had carried on rioting that day in November. Christopher Ponting was a defendant in a subsequent case, along with James Carver, John Draper, Charles Gillett and William Sparrow. They were charged with riotously assembling at Fairford on 26 November and destroying a chaff-cutting machine belonging to Joseph Jenkins. Their case was slightly different to the others, in that the law referred only to the destruction of threshing machines being felonious. The destruction of a chaff-cutting machine was not subject to as strict a punishment as a threshing machine, but the men were all found guilty.

Various punishments were meted out to the rioters and machine breakers in the Cotswolds. The lucky ones received discharges; others received prison sentences of between six months and three years. The more unfortunate ones were transported to Australia for up to fourteen years.

At the start of the assizes, the judge had called all the accused misguided and ignorant men, whose destruction of the threshing machine had been premeditated. He argued that if the men had started with the threshing machine, would they then move on to destroy humbler garden implements, or the weaving loom? As was sadly common with the more affluent members of society, the judge looked more at the aesthetics of Britain rather than at the economics. He argued that destroying these industrial inventions would destroy the livings of those who lived in rural areas. He also believed that all classes depended on each other, and therefore to ruin something of one class would impact on all the others, and therefore break up society. The middle and upper classes were always concerned to maintain the status quo and keep the working classes in their place, and the trial judge was no different. Although he recognized that the farm labourer was worse off than the farmer who would be left impoverished, allegedly, by the destruction of his threshing machine, he added that this was because the farmer would now have less money to help his employees. Yet some of Britain's farmers had actually increased their workers' poverty by reducing their wages in the assumption that the parish would make up the shortfall through out-relief – something that did not always happen. The judge's comments merely served to show the gulf between rich and poor in the nineteenth century Cotswolds, and further fuel resentment amongst the agricultural workers.

# CHAPTER 9

# 'Your Mother is Dead': Murdered by a Madman

## 1864

Sarah Alexander had married Richard Smith for better or for worse. But in their twenty-eight or so years of married life, there had been many 'worse' occasions. She thought she had married well; the daughter of a Berkshire agricultural labourer, she had married a respectable, middle class surgeon, the brother of a solicitor and wealthy farmer. She had been able to live in some comfort, wherever she had moved with her husband's practice -Winchcombe, Devon, Lambeth, then back to Winchcombe, where she and her husband lived on North Street. As was common for a Victorian wife, in the days before contraception, and with Queen Victoria as a role model, Sarah had soon become the mother to a large family, having nine healthy children.

But Richard Smith had a dark side to him that his wife had soon discovered. The successful doctor also had a long family history of insanity – and he was the latest member of the Smiths to suffer from periods of madness. Poor Sarah lived with his 'eccentric' spells and occasional incarcerations in lunatic asylums – but eventually, Richard's madness cost her her life.

Richard Smith was from a Winchcombe family, born around 1815 in the town. Of his siblings, two came to play a large part in his life – his brother William, three years his senior, and his sister Ann, born in 1811. The family had obviously had some money; in adulthood, Ann, a spinster, was listed in the censuses as a landed proprietress, and left her house –

Gloucester House on Gloucester Street in Winchcombe – to her niece Mary Elizabeth when she died. William was the owner of a substantial farm in Winchcombe, and was also a solicitor.

So the Smiths were middle-class and financially solvent. But there was also that history of insanity. Two of Richard's uncles were reported to have been mad, and one of his sisters had been incarcerated in Gloucester County Lunatic Asylum in the mid 1830s. This genetic insanity was also apparent in Richard. He had been sent to Gloucester County Lunatic Asylum in 1833, aged only eighteen, although it is doubtful whether Sarah knew this when she married Richard.

On one occasion, Richard had threatened to turn one of his brothers out of his house for no reason; and on another occasion had broken the windows in his sister Ann's house – and these had been taken as examples of his mental state. In 1846, he had had what the Victorians termed 'brain fever', and had nearly died as a result.

By 1851, the Smiths were living in Moreton Hampstead, near Newton Abbot in Devon. One night whilst he was living there, Richard had developed an obsession that a sign-board opposite his house was, in fact, a camera, and that someone was using it to take photos of his family inside the house. He therefore drew all the curtains in the house – both at the front and back – and kept them drawn for days so that no one could see in. On another day, he sharpened some knives, as a result, he said, of being able to hear a cat's meat seller sharpening his own knife … on London Bridge.

In Devon, Richard was also known for walking around the streets without a collar (obviously not a done thing in mid-Victorian England) and with his house slippers on. He would also sometimes take his fishing rod and attempt to fish in the middle of the road. It was said that periods of behaviour like this had stretched over the previous fourteen years.

In December 1852, his family was so concerned that Richard was examined by a doctor, to ascertain the state of his mind. This Dr Shapter decided that Richard suffered from chronic insanity, and was liable to attacks of acute insanity. Despite this diagnosis, Richard must have been able to carry on with normal life at various points; whilst in Devon, his wife gave birth to their last child, Clara, before the family moved on to south London. Richard was also still practising as a surgeon both in Devon and in London – surely something he would not have been able to do if his madness had been either constant or too invasive on his daily life.

The couple were living with youngest daughter Clara at 9 Cleve Place, Lambeth by 1861, but must have returned to Richard's hometown of Winchcombe soon after the census was taken. The children had dispersed by this point. Daughter Martha was living with her Uncle William on his farm in Winchcombe; Mary, Cornelius and William were staying with their Aunt Ann in Gloucester Street, Winchcombe; son Thomas was working as a flour mill bookkeeper and in lodgings at the flour mill, which was in Castle Street, Winchcombe; daughter Sarah Jane was at school in Cheltenham, and son James Adolphus was at a commercial school in Northleach. Why some of the children were living with relatives is not clear. Perhaps they had had enough of their father's 'eccentric' episodes and had chosen to move out – or concerned relatives had encouraged them to – or maybe they had just not wanted to move to London and so had chosen to return to their family's home.

Richard Smith had once been fairly affluent – but as his madness progressed, he was forced to stop work, and the money began to dry up. He had, by 1864, become reliant on his brother William for financial help, and his lodgings were more humble than he was used to. He rented a house in North Street in Winchcombe, which had once been one larger property but had been divided into two. The other half was now occupied by the Greenhalf or Greenhalgh family. The former surgeon, symbol of respectable, middle-class society, lived next door to a local wheelwright.

By December 1864, Mary, Cornelius and William were still living with Ann Smith, and Martha with William Smith. However, they saw their parents regularly. On 27 December, James, Cornelius and William had spent the afternoon at their parents' home on North Street. Their parents were still on affectionate terms – Sarah seems to have deeply loved her

*North Street, Winchcombe – home of the Smith family.* The author

husband, despite his mad spells and his lack of money in recent years – and the family spent a pleasant afternoon that Tuesday. The children left at different times – Cornelius at 6.00 pm, William at 6.30, and James the last to leave at 8.30 pm. When they left, their parents were still on good, friendly terms.

At about 9.00 pm, Mrs Greenhalf, the wheelwright's wife, was sitting down in her house, in a room that adjoined the Smiths' parlour, where Richard and Sarah usually sat in their leisure moments. Mrs Greenhalf heard a gun fire – but seems to have thought no more about it, and did not investigate.

The following morning, Mrs Wharton, a local charwoman, went to the Smiths' house, as she usually did, for some milk. Richard answered the door, but said nothing. Mrs Wharton asked how Sarah was – but received no reply.

Shortly after Mrs Wharton's visit, Richard walked to his brother William's farm and knocked on the door. It was answered by his son James. Richard asked where his sister Martha was; James answered that she had not yet come down from her bedroom. Richard then abruptly told him that his mother was dead. 'How?' asked a shocked James. Richard said something about a gun; but James, traumatized by his father's statement, could not take in exactly what he said. He hurriedly called to his brother William, and Richard repeated that Sarah was dead. William started out for North Street, but Richard called to him that it was no use going there, as his mother was definitely dead.

Richard then left William to go to North Street, and himself walked to Gloucester Street. On reaching Gloucester House, his sister Ann's home, he told Cornelius and Mary that their mother had died.

In the meantime, William had reached his parents' house, and on walking into the parlour, found his mother lying on her side on the floor. Her feet were towards the fireplace, and her head towards the door. One hand was stretched out, clinging onto a chair. She had obviously been dead for quite a few hours.

Mr Newman, a local surgeon, was called for, and found that Sarah had been shot in the neck, close to the base of the skull. He thought that the gun used must have been in a horizontal position to the wound when it was fired.

People didn't have to look very far to find the weapon. On the Tuesday afternoon when he had visited his parents, Cornelius had taken with him a gun from his uncle's farm, and had left it – loaded – in the corner of his parents' kitchen. A policeman soon found it, in the same position – but with the right-hand barrel discharged.

Richard had told Cornelius, when he visited him at Gloucester House, that the gun had been in his hand, and it had gone off, shooting Sarah; but when his son asked whether the gun had gone off accidentally, Richard made no answer.

When the police questioned locals about the affair, more strange tales of Richard's delusions and madness were revealed. Richard was under the belief that the police wanted to murder his family at the local police station, and would try and get them there by making false charges against them. When James had left his father's house on Tuesday evening, Richard begged him to run back to the farm in case the police

*Prison entry for Richard Smith. Gloucestershire Archives* (ref Q/Gc6/4)

caught up with him. He also believed his sons were going to be kidnapped and sent to fight in the war in America.

Richard was charged with the wilful murder of Sarah Smith on 28 December 1864, and his entry in the Gloucester Calendar of Prisoners stands out. Many of the other entries for this period are for agricultural labourers, often charged with thefts, most illiterate, with only a smattering of people able to read, and fewer able to write. But Richard's entry shows a surgeon with superior reading and writing skills, charged with the worst crime of all.

Richard was tried at the Spring Assizes in Gloucester on April Fool's Day, 1865. His brother, sister, eldest daughter, brother-in-law, and one of his sons were called to give evidence – and their evidence painted a vivid picture of a man with a long history of mental illness, from a family with a genetic tendency towards madness.

Richard's defence stressed that, given the good relationship between Richard and Sarah, he may well have fired the gun accidentally – perhaps as he brought the gun into the parlour for some reason. But the defence also pointed out that Richard's state of mind was an important factor. Richard was seen to be coherent and sensible after the murder, capable of holding a conversation – but he had refused to comment about the murder, and had no motive for killing his wife. Not surprisingly, given the evidence, the jury took little time to acquit Richard Smith of murder, on the grounds of insanity.

It was ruled that Richard should be kept indefinitely in Gloucester Gaol 'until Her Majesty's pleasure be known', and so he was a prisoner there for a year. He was discharged on 10 May 1865, on a warrant from the Home Secretary, and sent to

Broadmoor Lunatic Asylum, where he stayed for the rest of his life. He died there in 1883.

Richard Smith's children followed different paths to their father, apparently free from the mental illness that wrecked his life. His eldest daughter Mary inherited her spinster aunt's house and property, which enabled her to live a long life as a landed proprietor, and also freed her financially to stay single. In 1891, she had three of her nephews, the sons of her sister Martha, staying with her. They were medical and natural science students at university – but were all natives of Brisbane. For shortly after her mother's murder, Martha had emigrated to Australia, where she married a Scotsman and settled. Her sons became, variously, a GP, a surgeon, a geologist, and a civil engineer – and one of her grandsons, Donald Alastair Cameron, became Australian health minister and received the OBE. Whatever problems Richard might have had, he certainly didn't pass them on to these descendants!

# CHAPTER 10

# 'I Was Caught in the Trap': Arsenic in Daddy's Tea

## 1858

Ann Ind was typical of many women in the Cotswolds, whose lives were governed by the needs of the men in their lives.

Ann was born Ann Goodall in Quenington in 1829, and christened there on 20 December. She was the second youngest child of Joseph and Anne (her younger sister died in infancy, leaving her the youngest survivor) and had several siblings, born between 1813 and 1833.

Ann's mother died in 1848, in her fifties. She left, not Ann, but her sister Hannah, ten years her senior, as housekeeper to Joseph. Hannah remained with her father until she married at the late – for then – age of thirty-one. She married a twenty-nine-year-old widower from Fairford, Giles Marshall, in 1852. Did Hannah feel that she had looked after her father for long enough, and want a bit of happiness for herself? Marrying a widower was not the obvious choice, but as she was in her thirties, she may have opted for a safe bet. And Giles had no children from his first marriage, so it was only her husband she needed to look after now. Interestingly, Giles Marshall had a past. In 1851, he was listed in the census as a prisoner at Northleach House of Correction. Did Hannah marry an ex-con in order to escape the drudgery of looking after an elderly parent? Her younger sister now came to take her job as her father's carer, and Hannah went on to have a son with Giles, Edwin, born in 1855.

By the age of seventeen, Ann was working as a servant for Elizabeth Dakins and her daughter in Leckhampton. Later, she worked for Charles Price in Quenington and was described as a labourer. She probably worked on the fields in some capacity – she lived in a rural area, and the male members of her family were employed in agricultural professions (her brother Thomas was a shepherd, and her father also worked for Mr Price as an agricultural labourer).

Ann was a petite woman, about five feet one and a half in height, and pleasant to look at, with dark brown hair, blue eyes and a fresh complexion. She attracted the attentions of a local labourer, William Ind, known as Bill, and on 5 February 1856, aged twenty-five according to the records, Ann married thirty-one-year-old Bill Ind at Quenington. But she was not free; her husband was a poorly-paid labourer, and the young married couple had to live with Ann's father, sharing his cottage in Quenington with him. Ann and her father also worked as labourers, and their incomes became vital when William found himself out of work.

There was no sign that she had quarrelled with her father, but something caused her to go into Fairford on 5 January 1858 and visit the chemist shop owned by Mr Butler. His assistant, Henry Manning, who had known Ann before her marriage, served her. Ann asked for sixpence worth of arsenic – enough money for two ounces – to kill some rats. Manning was concerned; wouldn't she like to purchase the safer rat killer that was available, Phillip's Vermin Killer? Ann refused. Manning tried to further dissuade her by telling her that anyone who bought the poison had to sign a register; but Ann answered that she had no objection to signing. Manning accordingly sold Ann the arsenic, and she signed the register. But when Manning looked at her signature later, he found that she had signed in the name of Ann James.

On Thursday 7 January, when Joseph Goodall returned from work, he found Ann already in the house, having put the teapot on the table for him. His daughter said she had emptied out the tea leaves from the last brew, and the pot was now clean. The Goodall habit was to use the tea leaves twice before emptying them out. Joseph made a fresh batch of tea and quickly drank over four cups in succession – he usually took four or five after a long day's work. But the tea didn't taste very nice, and before Joseph had finished his last cup, he began to get strong stomach pains. He went out and leant against the garden gate for a while, to see if that made him feel better; but on sitting back down inside, he again felt poorly. He went up to bed, and lay down on his right side, but soon, he began to feel that he was swelling up under his left arm, and had a hot taste in his mouth. He then began to vomit, rapidly and several times. It was 3.00 am before he fell asleep.

Just two hours later, Joseph was awake again, and needing to get ready for work. He called to William, his son-in-law, to get up and boil the kettle for him, then when he himself had got downstairs, he made another pot of tea using the tea leaves left from the night before. But again, as soon as he had drunk, he became ill and vomited. Although he struggled into work, he had to return after twenty minutes, and go back to bed. He spent the whole of the next day in bed.

Ann was present during the Thursday, and on Friday, Joseph had darkly hinted to her that he knew what had happened. 'I would not have any more tea out of the pot,' he told her, 'because I thought there was a trap set in it, and if there was, I was caught in it, and greatly wounded.' Ann answered, 'Why do you think that? There was no trap set in it.'

Joseph sent his son-in-law, William Ind, to a doctor for some medicine. William returned with a bottle containing six doses of medicine. Joseph took a couple of the doses.

At teatime on Saturday, Mr Cornwell, a local surgeon, visited, to make sure Joseph was now on the mend. After he had left, Ann and William Ind sat down for their supper. Ann then went upstairs and came back down with a shawl and bonnet, and the leftover medicine. 'It has not done you any good,' she told Joseph, and took it out of the house, adding that she should do nothing for her father. William followed her out of the house, and Joseph, by now very suspicious of his uncaring daughter, locked the door.

On Sunday morning, Joseph started to make his way to Fairford to get a policeman, but found he was not able to get there. Instead, he saw his employer, a Mr Price, and told him his suspicions, and Mr Price called Sergeant Cook from the police to his house, to see Joseph.

*Quenington village, home to Joseph Goodall and his daughter Ann Ind.* The author

After Joseph had told Cook his theory that Ann had poisoned him, Cook accompanied him home. Ann seems to have then returned home briefly, to offer her father some onion broth, and to give him three doses from the medicine bottle. She seems to have changed her mind about its efficacy. She then left the house again.

Cook caught up with Ann later on the Sunday, and she claimed to him that her father had been similarly ill before. He asked her whether she had bought any rat killer, but she denied all knowledge of it. But on the following day, Cook found Ann at the house of a neighbour, Mrs Webb, in Fairford, and found that she had had a change of heart. She asked Cook to accompany her to her father's house, and he agreed. When she saw her father, she burst into tears, and said, 'Forgive me, I did do it; I did put it in the teapot, but Bill does not know anything about it.'

Cook wondered out loud about searching the house again for the remainder of the arsenic, for Ann could not have used the full two ounces on her father or else he would definitely be dead. Ann replied that there was no point in searching the house again, as she had thrown the rest of the arsenic into the outside privy.

Ann asked Joseph to forgive her, admitting that she had bought arsenic and used it on him. She tried to explain that she had not poisoned him twice; she had put arsenic in the tea leaves on the Thursday, but her father had become ill again on Friday by re-using the old tea leaves rather than making a fresh brew. Her father, though, was unmoved by her delayed tears, and grimly said, 'The country must forgive you – for I cannot.'

Why Ann had poisoned her father was a mystery, although his ordering of his son-in-law to get up and boil the kettle at 5.00 am probably didn't endear the old man to the younger generation. Perhaps he was sharp and bossy towards her and William, and she had slowly grown to resent him. She cannot have been thinking rationally when she poisoned him, though – her false signing of the chemist's register was odd, as Henry Manning had known her for some time, and knew what her name was.

Ann was charged on 16 January 1858 with administering arsenic to Joseph Goodall, with intent to murder him. She was tried at Gloucester on 6 April, before Mr Baron Channell. The defence lawyer, Mr Sawyer, emphasized the lack of motive on Ann's part, the open manner with which she had bought the arsenic, and the kindness (however late) that Ann had shown to Joseph when he was ill. However, when he tried to excuse his poorly prepared defence, saying that he had been asked to represent Ann at short notice and had no one to help him prepare the papers, Ann became hysterical and had to be removed from the courtroom, with proceedings being suspended.

The jury duly found Ann guilty of giving her father the poison, but said they could not determine with what intent she had acted. The judge asked them with what intent Ann could have acted, if it was not for the purpose of murder. The jury then found her guilty, but with a strong recommendation to mercy.

The patriarchal judge, in passing sentence, called the crime 'heinous', 'odious', 'greatly aggravated by the fact that the person to whom the poison was administered was the prisoner's own father.' In Victorian society, crimes by women against their fathers or husbands were viewed with disgust, horror and shock. They were seen as crimes against society, against the natural order of things. In the past, the murder of a husband by a wife had been seen as petty treason, and the punishment was being burned at the stake. There had been one infamous case in Gloucester, not so far away, in the mid-eighteenth century, when Anne Williams had been found guilty of poisoning her husband, and duly burnt. The judge also drew attention to the fact that poisoning someone involved buying and preparing the poison, so it had to be a premeditated crime. Mr Baron Channell ordered that the sentence of death be recorded against Ann Ind.

But Ann wasn't executed. On the Secretary of State's warrant, her sentence was commuted to life in prison. She was initially sent to Millbank Prison in London, but thirteen years later, she was listed in the 1871 census as a prisoner at the women's prison in Woking, Surrey, which had opened just two years earlier. She is listed there as a married agricultural labourer, but her short marriage to William Ind was over in all but name. William didn't stay to look after his father-in-law; instead, he returned home to Avening and his mother's house, where he lived until her death in 1870. He then moved in with his brother Richard – despite the latter already sharing his house with his wife and eleven children. He died in his hometown in 1881, still separated from his wife.

Joseph Goodall remained alone now in his cottage in Quenington. He was still living there in 1871, aged eighty. He had been born in the village in the last decade of the eighteenth century, and he was to die here too, later the same year. Luckily for him, his death was not at the hand of his daughter, Ann; but her actions may have put him off his multiple cups of tea for life.

# CHAPTER 11

# Too Young to Die: The Murder of Emily Gardner

## 1871

Some cases seem so modern that it is hard to believe they didn't happen yesterday. Some motives for crime have been the same throughout history – love, hate, jealousy, all feelings that can cause people to commit horrific acts today. In 1871, one case motivated by love and jealousy roused the attention of the national media. It was notable for several reasons, but when I read the first-hand account of it, I was struck by how modern it sounded.

Frederick Richard Jones was Cheltenham born and bred. The youngest son of a local stonemason, Henry Jones, and his wife Elizabeth, he was brought up at 36 Swindon Place, Cheltenham, with his two brothers, Henry and Edward. His brothers both started work as masons in their mid teens, but Frederick became apprenticed to a baker in Northfield, a suburb of Birmingham.

Frederick was illiterate and was considered by locals to be ignorant and appear younger than he was. He was only five foot three and a half, so his shortness may have added to this perception of youth. His father was also regarded as having little parental control over Frederick. However, by December 1871, Frederick was home from Birmingham and living again with his parents at 36 Swindon Place.

He had probably been back in Cheltenham for a few months by then, as he had started seeing a local girl, Emily Gardner. She was seventeen and a dressmaker, popular with boys and confident of her looks.

Emily's father, Peter, had originally been a blacksmith, but by 1871 was the landlord of the *Early Dawn* inn on the High

Street in Cheltenham. He lived there with his wife Sarah and his five children – Matilda (who died, aged fifteen, in 1867), Emily, Alice, Annie and John. They were a working-class family, and the children all worked from a fairly early age. John followed his father into smithing; Emily and Annie were both dressmakers; Alice went into service.

Frederick had been 'seeing' Emily for a few months, and was a regular at her father's pub. During the coroner's inquest on 11 December 1871, Peter Gardner recalled that Jones had been in the *Early Dawn* during the afternoon of the 10 December, for several hours. He said he had seen him at both tea and supper times, and both times thought he had been drinking, although he wasn't drunk. He added that Frederick drank beer nearly every day. Henry Jones, Frederick's father, went further, saying that the *Early Dawn* had ruined his son, and that over half his earnings each week were spent in that pub.

In the evening of 10 December, after drinking at the *Early Dawn*, Frederick, Emily and Alice Gardner moved onto *The Tiger* pub and shared a pint of beer. Alice then needed to return to her workplace, so Frederick and Emily accompanied her. Alice said that, until that day, they had all been good friends – and even on that day, she noticed no difference in him. However, Frederick Jones was a young man who suffered from jealousy. He was 'passionately' in love with Emily, but was sure that she had been 'intimate' with other men, and after they saw Alice to her residence, he decided to confront her about this. He later said that he had planned to confront her all day; and so had taken a razor belonging to Emily's father during the afternoon, with the intention of killing her if she refused to stop seeing other men.

Peter Gardner kept the razor on the wallplate over the kitchen window at the *Early Dawn*. Peter thought that Frederick had seen him use the razor, and that he had probably known where it was kept, as most of his family did.

Alice was in service at Saxham Villas in Cheltenham. The threesome – Alice, Emily and Frederick left the *Early Dawn* at 9.30 pm to walk to Saxham Villas; then Frederick walked Emily back to a small lane behind Wellington Square, which

*Houses on Wellington Square, Cheltenham – Emily Jones was murdered in a lane behind the square.* The author

they reached around 10.00 pm. He asked Emily whether she cared for him or not, to which she answered that she would do what she liked. Frederick threatened to kill her with her father's razor unless she told him whether she cared for him, and added that he didn't care if he was hanged for it. Understandably, Emily became scared, crying, 'Murder! Murder! Murder!' But it was too late. Frederick slit her throat, virtually decapitating her. He calmly dragged her body across the lane before walking back to his father's house, reaching there by 10.30 pm.

Frederick made no attempt to deny what he had done; in fact, his first words to poor Henry Jones were that he had murdered Gardner's daughter, and to go and tell Peter Gardner that. And when Police Constable Clayfield arrived to arrest him, Frederick told him he'd done it. PC Clayfield asked, 'Done what?' Frederick replied that he had murdered Emily, and told him where her body was – before filling up his pipe with tobacco for a smoke.

Both to his father and to PC Clayfield, Frederick suggested that a cut on his face was caused by Emily pulling the razor out from her pocket and injuring him. But he did not try to suggest that he killed Emily in self-defence; merely that she hurt him before he murdered her, as he had always intended to do.

Frederick – whilst calmly filling his pipe – had told PC Clayfield where he had put the body. He had hidden it in a ditch down the dark lane, in order that the body would not be run over by any carriages. Later, the missing razor blade was found near Emily's muff, when it fell off her right arm as the police moved her body.

Both Frederick and his father Henry said that drink had a lot to do with Frederick's crime. It exacerbated his jealousy and it is no wonder that Frederick referred to it as the 'accursed drink'. Sober, he confessed freely to the crime, and worried about the impact of it on his family, crying that he was going to break his poor mother's heart.

The only hole in his story was the suggestion that Emily had taken her father's razor and had cut Frederick's face in a temper before he killed her. Mr Jessop, a Cheltenham doctor, said there were no signs of a struggle between the two and that the wound on Frederick's cheek was so superficial it must have been self-inflicted.

Frederick Jones was charged with the murder of Emily Gardner and tried at Gloucester just before Christmas. His defence counsel argued that no motive had been found for the crime, and that the probability was that Emily had been the one to take the razor in the first place. He believed that Frederick had made 'too familiar advances' on Emily and that she had taken out the razor to repel him. He had then become irritated and attacked her. The defence argued that this would mean manslaughter, not murder. But the jury decided, after only a short deliberation, that Frederick was guilty of wilful murder. The judge sentenced him to death, and Frederick was said to have been completely overcome by the pronouncement.

Here, things take a slightly unusual turn. One might have expected public sympathy to have lain entirely with Emily Gardner and her family; and for people to despise, or hate, the illiterate baker who slit her throat. Yet there seems to have been a lot of sympathy for Frederick Jones.

The Home Secretary at the time, Henry Bruce, Lord Aberdare, received petitions from many locals asking that the death sentence on Frederick be commuted to life imprisonment. Banbury MP, industrialist and educationist, Bernhard Samuelson, was asked by his son, Henry Bernhard Samuelson, the Cheltenham MP, to pass on a letter to Bruce asking for the reduced sentence. Samuelson Senior added that he was sure the Home Secretary would consider every argument that would recommend Frederick 'to the mercy of the Crown'.

An H Hall of 359 Old Kent Road wrote to the Home Secretary on 3 January 1872, summing up many people's views on Frederick. He asked for any extenuating circumstances to be taken into account, as he was still just a 'lad'.

Manchester resident Charlotte Jones – Frederick's aunt or sister-in-law – was another person who wrote to the Home Secretary on 3 January. She commended Richard's father to him, saying that he was an honest, upright, hardworking stonemason who had never previously been near a court. She added that Richard himself was young and of good character, and that it had not been proved 'by whom the weapon was first introduced', and so these circumstances should be looked at and his sentence mitigated, if possible.

On 2 January, a petition signed by fifty-eight local people (as diverse as ministers, tailors and 'eating house keepers'!) was presented to both Stroud MP Henry Winterbotham and to the Home Secretary by Cheltenham solicitor W Edward Smith. In commending the petition to Winterbotham's attention, Smith said that there was no evidence of premeditation, and doubt as to whether Frederick or Emily had taken Peter Gardner's razor. He added that Frederick appeared far younger than his years, and had not had much of an education.

The petition asked for Frederick to be granted a reprieve on several grounds. Firstly, there was no evidence of premeditation; secondly, he made no effort to abscond or hide what he had done; thirdly, it was likely that Emily had taken

*The petition to stop Frederick Jones from being hanged – it failed. The National Archives* (ref HO 45-9286-9315 (8) p5)

the razor from her father's kitchen rather than Frederick; and fourthly, a few minutes before the murder, Emily and Frederick had appeared on good terms, suggesting that there was again no premeditation; fifthly, that two witnesses who claimed to have heard Frederick shouting were 158 yards away from him and so could not have heard him very accurately. In addition, Henry Jones had not been questioned for long

*Several people witnessed the execution of Frederick Jones. Their signatures are on this document to prove his death.* The National Archives (ref HO 45-9296-9315 (13))

enough at the trial, when he could have provided evidence that Frederick had not previously had the razor. A final plea for a reprieve focused on Frederick's personal qualities. His age, appearance, ignorance, lack of schooling, and the fact that, apparently, his parents had not controlled him very much in his youth, were apparently grounds for lenience.

It can be seen that the grounds the petitioners had for calling for a reprieve for Frederick were very slight, basically amounting to 'he's too young to die', it probably being a spontaneous act (despite Frederick's previous assertion that he had intended to kill Emily), and doubt about who had taken the razor from Peter Gardner's pub. But the fact remained that Frederick HAD murdered Emily Gardner, out of simple jealousy.

The petition and the letters to the Home Secretary, perhaps unsurprisingly, failed to secure any change to Frederick's sentence. On Monday 8 January 1872, Frederick Jones was executed by William Calcraft in Gloucester Gaol's yard. It was the first private hanging in the country, so at least Frederick was afforded some privacy rather than the madness of a public spectacle. He had to climb steps to reach the platform, as the scaffold was raised some four or five feet high – not much less than Frederick's height. He was executed at 8.00 am and his body buried the same evening in the Gaol Yard Enclosure. He was one month short of his twenty-first birthday.

# CHAPTER 12

# Panicking Convicts: The Perils of Poaching

## 1833

The Cotswolds have been home to intrepid poachers for centuries. Wealthy landowners have ensured that large pieces of the countryside have remained officially out of reach to the local population, whilst filling their land with pheasants and grouse for them and their friends to shoot for fun. It is no wonder that many of the local working population have resented the fact that the land around them, whilst full of things to catch, eat or sell on, has been inaccessible to them, and have tried to do something about it.

There are many stories about local poachers trying to catch birds from estates in order to feed themselves and their families. These men, hard up, deserve our sympathy. Others, equally poor, have caught birds in order to sell them on and receive a few pennies – again, fair enough. But the Cotswolds have also been home to opportunists, career poachers, who have poached birds not out of necessity but out of greed.

Giles Coates was one man who raided a Cotswold estate, a man with a bad reputation who didn't care who crossed his path whilst he was out looking for birds.

Giles was a Chedworth man, who worked as a clock and watch maker. However, locals also knew him to be a professional poacher, and an idle, dissolute character who wanted to make his fortune without working too hard for it. He was born in Chedworth in 1783, the son of Giles and Jane. In 1805, he had married Sarah Restall in Northleach. His was a respected Chedworth family; his father was a skilled

*View of Chedworth Woods, where George Simper worked, and was shot.* The author

clockmaker and his grandfather was a land surveyor and active member of the local community.

Sarah and Giles Coates had five children between them, Giles, Marianne, William, John and Eliza being born between 1806 and 1819. Giles was an average looking man, being about five feet five or six, quite stout, with grey hair. He looked like any other middle-aged man and father. But he was still recognisable to many from a distance, as he was round-shouldered, and had a distinctive stooping walk.

A large part of the local area came under the estate of Lord Stowell, a successful barrister. Stowell Park was two miles from Northleach, but covered thousands of acres on both sides of the river Coln, being a mix of grassland, arable and woodland, and including Chedworth Woods. Its main estate village was Yanworth. Lord Stowell employed a variety of people to look after his estate, including a gamekeeper – George Simper.

George was only two years older than Giles Coates. He had been born in Wiltshire, but was in Chedworth by the time he married another Wiltshire native, Mary Shergold, in 1809. His children – Louisa, Thomas, Jane, Esther and Althea – were all born and raised on the Stowell Park estate. George was a family man, a decent, respectable man working hard for his employer to protect his land and assets. Unfortunately, that didn't matter to someone like Giles Coates.

Although Giles had a profession, it seems to have been poaching that really appealed to him. It wasn't that he was poor and needed to poach in order to feed his family; but he was able to sell on what he caught and make some extra money. The thrill of knowing he might be caught himself at any moment may have also appealed. He was certainly known to be a regular poacher amongst his neighbours.

On the night of 20 October 1833, Giles Coates went out into Chedworth Woods to see what he could poach. George Simper was on duty in the area that night, and duly heard shots from within the wood. Realizing it was poachers, he followed the noise, and soon came across Giles. He managed to confront Giles, and after some arguing, took the stock of Giles's double-barrelled gun away from him. But Giles knew how to work his gun, and struck the percussion cap with a knife, thus discharging it. George was hit in the side, seriously injuring him.

Giles, in a panic, fled on foot, leaving the unfortunate George Simper lying on the ground on a cold autumn night, until he was discovered and carried home. He was examined, and it was found that his injuries were so serious that he was likely to die sooner rather than later.

Meanwhile, Giles had escaped detection. Realizing that George Simper knew who he was – after all, they were both locals, of around the same age, and had grown up together – he knew that he could not stay in Chedworth. He chose to flee to London, where he was unknown and could stay anonymous. As a precaution, he chose to disguise his appearance, probably by growing a beard and whiskers.

But Giles had not reckoned on the publicity that would be generated by George's injuries. A reward of £50 was soon offered for information, and handbills printed advertising the fact. These handbills seem to have had a wide circulation; but

## Fifty Pounds Reward.

WHEREAS, on the Evening of Sunday, October the 20th, GEORGE SIMPER, Gamekeeper to the Right Hon Lord Stowell, at Chedworth, in the county of Gloucester, while endeavouring to secure GILES COATES, of Chedworth aforesaid whom he detected in a Wood, in the unlawful pursuit of Game was DELIBERATELY FIRED AT, within the distance of one yard, and severely wounded in the side, by the said Giles Coates, who immediately absconded, leaving behind him a short double-barrelled gun and his hat.

Whoever will apprehend the said Giles Coates, or cause him to be apprehended and lodged in any of his Majesty's Gaols, shall receive the above Reward of FIFTY POUNDS on application to Mr. Daniel Glover, of Chedworth, Woodward; or to Messrs. Pearce and Kent, Solicitors, Craig's Court, Charing Cross, London.

The said GILES COATES is by trade a Watchmaker, about 50 years of age, 5 feet 5 or 6 inches high, stout made, dark complexion, and hair rather inclined to grey, round shouldered, and stoops in his walk.—Cirencester, October, 1833.

*The advert placed in the local press after Giles Coates fled to London.* Gloucestershire Archives (Gloucester Journal, 2/11/1833)

to make sure the reward received the maximum publicity, an advert was put in the newspapers, stating that the reward was offered to 'whoever will apprehend the said Giles Coates, or cause him to be apprehended and lodged in any of his Majesty's Gaols'.

In the meantime, James Hall, previously a policeman based at Bow Street in London, but now a farmer staying with his father in Northleach, was also acting as a parish constable. He was told to try and follow Giles Coates in order to take him into custody. Perhaps Giles had made the mistake of telling people where he was going; or perhaps it was guessed that he would go to the capital. Whichever way, James Hall followed Giles straight to London.

James did not have a warrant for Giles' apprehension, but was simply looking for him. But London then, as now, was a large city, and James at first had no luck in spotting the absconding poacher. But in November 1833, after a month on the run, Giles's luck ran out. One night, he was walking along either Whitehall or Cockspur Street (depending on which newspaper you read), when James Hall happened to walk past him. James immediately recognized Giles, despite the latter's attempts to change his appearance. James seized Giles, and told him why he was wanted. Giles then made a desperate bid to escape, by trying to bribe James to the tune of £5. Honest James refused. Giles then asked if James would come with him to Giles's son's house. Giles Junior, then aged twenty-eight, was working as a clockmaker in Pall Mall. Giles said his son would be able to give James £10. James again refused, and marched Giles to Bow Street Police Station. There, he was taken into custody. He refused to say anything more.

The case being heard in Gloucestershire, Giles was taken from London to Gloucester for his trial at the 1834 Lent Assizes. Unsurprisingly, he was found guilty of attempting to murder George Simper, and was sentenced to death on 29 March. But although Giles did die as a result of his crime, it was not under the hangman's noose. At his trial, the judge said that he had decided to spare Giles's life, although the decision had granted the judge a lot of worry. But although the judge may have fretted about making the right decision, he had decided to reprieve Giles, and the latter instead received a sentence of transportation to Australia.

On 12 December 1834, Giles Coates left his family for the last time, and sailed off in the convict ship *George The Third* en route to a new life alone in the colonies. But the *George The Third*, which was carrying over 200 prisoners, was blighted. The convicts were locked up for the majority of the day in their cells, which were below decks and thus in the dark. Their diet would have been plain, and lacking in fresh fruit or vegetables. It was no surprise, then, that scurvy broke out among the prisoners during the voyage, killing several of them. No sooner had the others recovered from that, than disaster struck. The convict transportation registers tell the story in blunt terms, stating that the ship was wrecked after striking a rock in the mouth of the River Derwent on 12 April 1835. After a long journey and numerous privations, the ship had almost reached Hobart in Tasmania when it was wrecked.

Although some survived the wrecking, it was mainly the ship's crew and prison warders who lived; less than half the convicts survived. The convicts had been locked up in their cells when the accident happened, and so were unable to escape. Stories also circulated that the crew refused to help the panicking convicts when it became clear that the ship would sink, and left them to their fate. The transportation registers are a sad record of the convicts' fate. Annotated in pencil next to each name in the register is a note of what happened to them in the accident. Next to Giles Coates' name is one word – 'Drowned'. He was killed as a result of the shipwreck; was this divine retribution for the life Giles had tried to destroy back in Chedworth?

News, even in that day and age, travelled fast. His wife, Sarah, was informed of her husband's death, but instead of retiring from society in grief for her husband, she instead got on with her life. Two years after Giles's death, she married local labourer John Moss.

Giles Coates lost his life as a result of his crime; but George Simper didn't. His was a happier ending. Despite the local media's reports that George had received very serious injuries and was in imminent danger of dying, and it later being reported that he was still lying in a 'dangerous' state, he in fact survived another twenty-four years, dying in Yanworth on 7 August 1858, aged seventy-seven.

# CHAPTER 13

# 'A Very Idle and Disorderly Fellow': Abduction of a Minor

## 1867

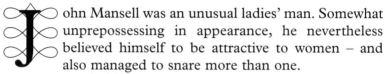ohn Mansell was an unusual ladies' man. Somewhat unprepossessing in appearance, he nevertheless believed himself to be attractive to women – and also managed to snare more than one.

He was also a man who believed in taking a woman by force if she didn't respond to him; a violent man with a bad reputation in his hometown of Stow-on-the-Wold.

John Mansell was born in 1839 in Stow, and worked as a ratcatcher or labourer, depending on where there was work. He wasn't tall – just five feet four and a half inches – but may have been attractive in his youth, with his hazel eyes and fresh complexion. He certainly managed to attract one girl's attention – Isabella White, a few years his junior, from Alderton. They married in Winchcombe in 1860, and settled into lodgings in Gloucester Street.

It was whilst living in Winchcombe that John seems to have first started committing crimes – or at least, first started being caught. In December 1861, he and one John Woodward were convicted of stealing a pair of women's cuffs, the property of Thomas Robson. Of course, this was in the age when a woman's possessions were automatically seen as being the property of her husband. Woodward had previously been in trouble with the police and so was given eight months' hard labour at Gloucester Gaol; this seems to have been John Mansell's first conviction, so he was given a lesser punishment – two months' imprisonment and hard labour. One of Mansell's fellow prisoners at Gloucester was Stow chimney sweep David Johns, who had been jailed for two years in December 1860 for assault. More on him later.

John's experience of Gloucester Gaol at twenty-years-old did nothing to deter him from further criminal activities. In October 1862, he was convicted of an assault, and sentenced to one month's hard labour. He was given the opportunity of avoiding prison if he paid £2 – but John chose prison, presumably because he could not afford the fine.

After John Mansell's release from his second stint in prison, he moved with his wife to Stow-on-the-Wold, and their son Joseph was born there in 1863. But John seems to have been a short-tempered individual with a penchant for using his fists. In March 1863, he was again convicted of an assault, and given a choice of two months' hard labour or a fine of £10. Unsurprisingly, given that he couldn't pay a £2 fine a year earlier, John was unable or unwilling to pay £10, and again returned to prison.

A year later, John was again in trouble with the law – but this time on a more serious charge. In 1864, he and his friend Jesse Smith, a sweep who, like John, was married with a child (and whose wife, Eliza, joined her husband in prison within a year, after being convicted of stealing two chemises, two sheets and a veil), were arrested on suspicion of unlawfully assaulting a woman named Maria Johns, 'with intent carnally to know her' – in other words, attempted rape. At the Quarter Sessions in Gloucester on 16 March 1864, both men were both found guilty of assault with intent to ravish (also referred to as criminal assault) and sentenced to two years' hard labour.

If Maria's name sounds familiar, it is because she was the wife of David Johns – the sweep who, at age sixty-one, had been one of John's fellow inmates at Gloucester Gaol in 1861. Maria and David had both been married before, with several children between them, and it is likely that their relationship started before the death of David's first wife Rosanna. Maria was, at the time of the attempted rape, in her fifties, but may have been seen as easy or fair game by John and Jesse because of her and her husband's reputations (like John, David was a regular offender, being convicted of various thefts and assaults between 1840 and 1874).

John had, by this time, acquired a reputation of his own around the Stow area. The Calendar of Prisoners of 1864 records him in unflattering terms, stating that from youth, he was a known thief and poacher and was a 'very idle and disorderly fellow'. Jesse Smith was named as an associate of Mansell's and of bad character.

Interestingly, more than a year after John's incarceration, his daughter Georgiana was born in Stow. There is no record of him having been released early from his sentence – was he allowed conjugal visits, or did the records fail to record an early release? Whatever the case, John was released and returned home to his wife and two young children.

John Mansell was released from prison at the end of 1866, but was by no means a reformed character. In fact, he seems to have been searching for more excitement in his life after his release, and, by 1867, he had started an affair with a teenager – Martha Williams. She was barely fifteen years old, and lived with her mother and step-father in Stow. John, at this time, was twenty-eight and married – and now, of course, a father of two.

Martha was illegitimate, and as such, her birth had not been registered by her mother. The courts therefore had difficulties in proving her age, and had to rely on the testimony of Eliza Williams, and also of the nurse who had attended Martha's birth.

Eliza had been concerned about Martha's relationship with Mansell for some time. She had warned her not to continue her intimacy with him – and her step-father, William Clapton, had indeed beaten her for continuing to see Mansell. But her mother might not have been a great role model – not only was Martha illegitimate, but her mother went on to have another two illegitimate children – Job and Hannah, neither being Clapton's child – before finally marrying Clapton, a plasterer's labourer, in 1870.

On 16 May 1867, Martha left Stow with Mansell and went with him to a place called Whitmarsh Hall, where he was working, and ended up living with him there for three weeks. Eliza Williams then called the police who arrested Mansell for unlawfully taking a minor out of the possession, and against the will, of her mother. Today, Mansell would probably have been arrested for unlawful intercourse; then, he was charged with abduction.

The defence at Mansell's court case argued that Martha had left home because her step-father was mistreating her, and not as a result of her relationship with Mansell. But the jury found Mansell guilty, and he was sentenced to three months' imprisonment with hard labour. Again, he seems to have left his wife Isabella pregnant at the time of his imprisonment, with William Mansell being born in 1868.

His record states that he was a 'very bad character', drunken, and had been accused previously of various offences including assaults and the attempted rape of 1864. Why young Martha found him attractive is a mystery – he is listed in both 1867 and 1871 as having a speech impairment and a crippled hip. She must have been attracted to his 'bad boy' image; and was also, perhaps, desperate for an excuse to leave home and her abusive step-father.

However, Mansell was never with Martha for very long – in 1868 and 1869 he had two more spells in prison for poaching and trespassing. And in 1871, his temper again got the better of him. Local police constable Edwin Shipton, who had known John and his reputation for ten years, had been trying to arrest him at Stow on 27 December 1871 – and John promptly tried to resist arrest and assaulted the policeman. The Calendar of Prisoners records that Mansell had already been in Gloucester Gaol for theft, rape and poaching. He was given six months' imprisonment at Gloucester, and was released on 3 July 1872.

Either Martha Williams was also of 'bad character' (as the Victorian law officials liked to put it) or John Mansell had corrupted the mind of the young woman he lived with. Whilst John was in prison in 1872, Martha herself was arrested and appeared in court, charged with:

*Keeping a certain common, ill-governed, and disorderly house, and causing men and women of evil name and fame to frequent the same, at Stow-on-the-Wold.*

So within a few years of starting a relationship with this older man of bad reputation, twenty-year-old Martha had become a

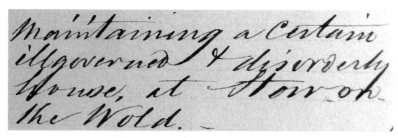

*Excerpt from Martha Williams' prison entry.* Gloucestershire Archives (ref Q/Gc6/6)

convicted madam of a local brothel. Interestingly, the Calendar of Prisoners calls her a 'labourer', whereas many other female prisoners in Gloucestershire around the same time are listed as prostitutes – so it seems Martha may have run the brothel, but not necessarily been a prostitute herself. But in John's absence, it was a way to make money – otherwise, there were not a lot of opportunities for an illiterate, poorly educated working-class woman at this time.

Martha was found guilty of 'unlawfully keeping a bawdy-house' and imprisoned for three months at Gloucester, starting in July 1872. Ironically, this is the month that John Mansell was released from prison – he was released the day after Martha was tried.

However, their consecutive spells in prison didn't put an end to their relationship. In 1870, she had given birth to Mansell's daughter, Emma, and the couple settled in Shepherds Row. By this time, Mansell's wife Isabella had moved on – but not very far. She had started a relationship with waterman Thomas Kendall, twenty years her senior, and was living next door to John and Martha. It wasn't possible, in the mid nineteenth century, for a couple like John and Isabella to divorce, so they continued to live with their new partners whilst still technically married. Isabella and Thomas had two illegitimate children – Fanny in 1877 and James in 1879 – but unlike John and Martha's children, they took their natural father's surname.

In 1874, Martha gave birth to John's second illegitimate child – John Mansell Williams. But John Mansell had lived fast and loose – and died young, at forty-one, in 1880.

The women in John Mansell's life reacted to his death in similar ways. Neither grieved over him for long. Martha was

*View along Shepherds Row, Stow, towards Sheep Street. Shepherds Row is where John Mansell and Martha Williams lived, next door to John Mansell's wife.* The author

too practical to mourn John – if indeed, their relationship had lasted until his death. Shortly after he had died, she married another local man – one George Cook. Around the same time, Mansell's widow, Isabella, married her long-term partner Thomas Kendall, and went on to have another two children by him. Her younger son by Mansell, William, took his stepfather's surname, although elder son Joseph stayed a Mansell.

But Martha's life was not to last long. She lived with George Cook and her two children by Mansell at 14 Well Lane, Stow, but was married for only three years before her death at the age of just thirty-one. They lived short lives – but made sure that there was never a dull moment in them.

# CHAPTER 14

# A Captain in the Bengal Infantry: The Cirencester Bigamist

# 1862

The Date family were innkeepers and hotel owners in Cirencester, a family who aspired to more than they had been born with, and who were ambitious for their children. They trained the children to run their bars, to be independent and capable, to hold their own in society.

Thomas Date, the patriarch, was originally from Birmingham, but was settled in Cirencester by 1838, when he married Wiltshire-born Elizabeth Banning. Thomas was a hotel or innkeeper, a family man who cared about his children. He and Elizabeth had seven children, all born in Cirencester – a lot of mouths for him to feed.

By 1851, Thomas Date was the innkeeper at the *King's Head* on Dyer Street in Cirencester. The inn was large enough to accommodate Thomas and Elizabeth, their children, a housemaid, waitress, boots, under-ostler, and three grooms. As the family had been in Cirencester for twenty years, and all the Date children had been born in the town, it is clear that they liked stability. That can also be seen from their long stewardship of the *King's Head* – unlike other establishments, that changed hands frequently, the Dates were running the *King's Head* from at least 1841 until 16 April 1862, when a dashing young army officer took lodgings with them.

The officer was one John Alexander Conroy, then aged about forty. He was a romantic soul, it seemed, for within a fortnight of moving into the *King's Head*, he had made it clear that he had fallen in love with Thomas Date's second daughter Jane, and he wrote her a love letter in which he declared his passion for he. He threatened to leave the *King's Head Hotel*

*The* King's Head, *Cirencester, home to the Date family.* The author

immediately if Jane said that she didn't feel the same way about him, and paid his bill to show his seriousness.

Poor Jane was only eighteen, and was bowled over by this older, experienced man who was expressing such strong feelings towards her. She talked with her friends, and decided to accept John's proposal. He was, from that point, considered one of the Date family.

John Conroy then announced that he had to return to his regiment in Calcutta in August 1862. He produced a letter which stated that a booking had been made on a P&O ship in the name of Captain and Mrs Conroy, to take them to Calcutta. Thomas Date, as a dutiful father, made inquiries as to Captain Conroy's past and respectability. First of all, he checked the annual Army List, but couldn't find the name of John Alexander Conroy there. He called Conroy's attention to this; but Conroy expressed surprise, and said that he would write to his friend, Sir John Lawrence, who would be able to vouch for him. He wrote the letter, and in a day or two, both Thomas and Conroy received letters supposedly from Sir John, vouching for the fact that Conroy was indeed a captain in the Bengal Infantry. The response was on paper marked 'On Her Majesty's Service', and it satisfied Thomas Date's doubts.

The Dates began to make arrangements for the wedding, which was to be a double wedding – Jane's sister Mary Elizabeth would be marrying her fiance, Henry Wigley, a Birmingham ironmonger, at the same time. Captain Conroy told the Dates that he wished to settle £200 a year on Jane, and in order to put that into writing, visited the Cirencester solicitors Messrs Mullings and Company, and asked them to prepare the necessary deeds. They wanted to know what property the captain had – in other words, how he proposed to finance Jane's settlement – and he arranged for a letter to be sent from a London stockbroker's, who had recommended investing in a certain stock, and reminded Captain Conroy that his funds amounted to £5,610.

This amount must have been a surprise to the Dates, as the captain had seemed short of money throughout his stay at the *King's Head*. On several occasions, he had borrowed small amounts of money from the hotel's waiters.

The night before the wedding, Conroy handed two cheques to Thomas Date. One was on plain paper, dated 9 June 1862, and drawn on Messrs Hopkinson and Company of Regent Street – it was for Captain Conroy, for the amount of £100. It was signed by a Major-General W L Davies – Conroy said this was his brother-in-law. The other cheque was in three pieces, which had been glued together with the edges of postage stamps. It was for £150, drawn on Messrs Prescott Grote and Company, and signed George J Graham. However, the date had been written over previous writing that had been erased, and was an obvious forgery.

But despite these hints that Conroy was not solvent, and so was not a perfect match for Jane Date, the marriages between Jane Cowley Date and John Alexander Conroy, and Mary Elizabeth Date and Henry Wigley went ahead on 9 July 1862, presided over by the Reverend Canon Powell, vicar of Cirencester. Conroy signed his name somewhat uncertainly, adding an extra 'r' to his surname – making it 'Conrory'. He gave his father's details as Alexander Frederick Conroy, gentleman, and his own occupation as British Diplomatic Service.

On the morning of the wedding, Conroy had found that he had lost his purse. As it couldn't be found after the wedding, when the happy couple were about to leave, Conroy asked Thomas Date if he could lend him some money to go on with. Conroy retrieved the £100 cheque from Thomas Date and sent it to the County of Gloucester Bank with Date's compliments. Coincidentally, the bank manager was Thomas Date's brother-in-law; so, not unreasonably, he cashed the cheque. Having received the money, and married Jane, Conroy left Cirencester with his new wife, promising to return within two weeks. Two days later, the cheque was found to be a fake. Then the men who had apparently written to Thomas Date testifying as to Conroy's character stated that the letters were forgeries. Then the second cheque was also found to be forged. Meanwhile, Jane Date, still in her teens, was on her honeymoon in Jersey with her glamorous army officer, oblivious to the investigations taking place in Cirencester.

The police were now involved and Edwin Riddiford, chief officer of police, traced Conroy to Jersey. He arrested him at *Bree's Hotel* and took him back to Cirencester. He was found to have with him four large travelling boxes and a large piece of wedding cake, addressed to Major-General Damer in

*The marriage entry for 'John Alexander Conroy' and Jane Cowley Date.*
Gloucestershire Archives (ref P/86/1/IN1/14)

Calcutta. In his pocket-book were thirty-six duplicates for jewellery and plate, pledged with various sellers from different parts of the country, but most dating from 1860. Captain Conroy seemed to be crestfallen, and have little to say. He was remanded in custody until his trial for forgery. He tried to get his wife to help him out of this dark spot, asking her to talk to her father on his behalf, as Mr Date was the only person who could save him.

Poor Jane must have been devastated to find out that her new husband was a forger who had tricked her, her father – in fact, her whole family. But the forgeries turned out to be the least of his deceits. For John Alexander Conroy was, it emerged, also hiding two other wives – neither of whom knew of Jane Date.

The subsequent police investigation revealed that Captain Conroy was, in fact, the more prosaically named James Summers, son of a London pawnbroker and silversmith, born in 1822 in the Finsbury area of north London. On 7 July 1847, at St Saviour Southwark, he had married Margaret Loudon, also the child of a silversmith, from Blackfriars Road in London, and they settled in the Shoreditch area, where James Summers, together with his brother-in-law, operated as an auctioneer. He and Margaret had four children together.

In 1859, Summers had deserted Margaret, leaving her to cope alone. But Margaret was an independent woman, and was able to cope well without her errant husband. In due course, Summers heard that Margaret was making a good living by letting out apartments – and so he returned to her. But in 1861, he again deserted her.

He then turned up as a lodger at the *Bridge House Hotel* in Windsor, where he stayed under the name of Captain Conroy. He soon made friends with twenty-one-year-old Emily Dawson Graham, the niece of the *Bridge House Hotel's* landlord – and on 11 January 1862, he married her. But only months later, he had moved on to Cirencester, and the Date family.

On 18 December 1862, one James Summers, alias John Alexander Conroy – now listed as a jeweller and exporter – was charged with three counts of bigamy and forgery. Most of the evidence regarded the forged cheques, and there wasn't much of a defence – the defence, as it was, relied on some small discrepancies in witness evidence. Not surprisingly, the jury found James Summers, alias John Conroy, guilty of forgery. The charge of bigamy was only then made, and Summers pleaded guilty to it. The judge made it clear that the forgery was the bigger crime, sentencing James Summers to 15 years' penal servitude just for that crime. He added that it was not necessary to sentence him for the bigamy.

But the three wives of James Summers – Margaret, the first and legal wife, and Emily and Jane, the young, innocent women seduced by the glamorous army officer – were left to pick up their lives. In Victorian England, they could have sunk under the embarrassment and talk about their bigamist husband. The court case had been incredibly popular with the public, who had crammed into court to hear the evidence. What happened to Emily Dawson Graham after James Summers was convicted is not known; but Margaret and Jane proved their worth as women who were not going to let a lying, cheating man get the better of them. Neither remarried, but neither slunk off into the sunset either. Margaret stayed in south London, living with her children, who seem, unsurprisingly, to have been close to their mother. She had to take in lodgers on occasion to get by, but managed. By 1881, she was describing herself as a widow.

Jane Cowley Date, scarred by her experience of men, remained single, and continued living with her mother after her father Thomas died in 1871. She followed in her family's footsteps, becoming a hotel keeper in Bristol and then in Weston-super-Mare. Her sister Mary, who married at the same time as Jane, had a longer marriage that resulted in at least eleven children – one wonders who was the luckier sister. James Summers' fate after his release from prison, though, remains unknown.

# CHAPTER 15

# 'We'll have no Czar of Russia Here': The Troublesome Vicar

# 1888

Thehe Hippisley family has had a link with Stow-on-the-Wold for centuries. Since John Hippisley bought the right to appoint the rector of St Edward's Church in Stow in the 1730s, several Hippisleys have been rector there, and many more have been born in the parish. But the local archives and papers are mainly concerned with the actions of one particular member of the family – the Reverend Robert William Hippisley, who was rector of Stow for nearly fifty-five years, yet never sought or achieved the respect or love of his parishioners. In fact, the locals' view of him can be summed up by the fact that at one point, he was so unpopular that an effigy of him was paraded through the streets of Stow.

Robert Hippisley was from a privileged background far removed from that of most of his parishioners. Born in 1818 at his family's estate at Lambourne in Berkshire, he was educated at Eton before going to Exeter College, Oxford, to study for his degree. Whilst at university, he met a Yorkshireman, Robert Raikes, and through him, his sister Grace Raikes. In 1841, aged just twenty-three, he married Grace.

Robert was ordained in 1840, and became rector of Stow in 1844, when still in his twenties, although one of his brothers, Henry, was formally the patron of St Edward's Church. The living was viewed as a good one; but unfortunately, the same could not be said of the church, which had become neglected during the time when Robert's grandfather, John, had been

*The peaceful setting of St Edward's Church, Stow, where Robert Hippisley was the strong-willed rector for some fifty years.* The author

rector (he died in 1822). The new rector decided that one of his first acts after coming to Stow had to be to restore the church – using much of his own money. He chose architect John Loughborough Pearson to repair the church – Pearson had also designed the Welsh home of one of Robert's brothers-in-law. Robert's decision to restore the church could be seen as either an act of charity and munificence to the local community – or as an act made out of a desire to immortalize himself as a generous man who saved this local church.

He was not a modest, retiring rector. In the late 1850s, he commissioned John Loughborough Pearson to design and build him a new house – Quarwood, off the Fosse Way just south of Stow. This Gothic pile was grand and palatial (and flamboyant enough to become home to a rock star nearly 150 years later, when The Who's John Entwistle bought it and lived in it until his death in 2002), and must have cost an enormous amount when it was first built. He seems to have split his time between Quarwood and the old rectory in Market Square, sometimes referred to as Church Green, as different censuses list him in different locations.

So Reverend Hippisley was a man who wanted to make an impression, to live a life of some luxury and be remembered after he died. He was opinionated and wanted to be involved in local decisions and the running of community establishments. However, his opinions were often in the minority, and he had a way of rubbing people up the wrong way.

To detail all the arguments that Robert got into with his parishioners would take a book of its own. However, one of the major issues he got involved with was to do with the Stow National School, which had been founded at Well Lane in the 1840s by the rector and his churchwardens after they acquired a charity estate, with Robert Hippisley as the school's manager. In the 1880s, though, a school board for the town and neighbouring Maugersbury was formed, and tensions arose between the board and the Rector. In 1887, the rector resigned as manager of the National School, and the school board took over its running, but this wasn't the end of the problems.

Prior to 1888, school children who were church-goers had attended a service at church at 9.00 am before going on to school. However, in this year, the school board decided to start school lessons at 9.00 am, meaning the children couldn't attend church. After hearing about this, the Rector made the purposely disruptive move of making the church service start at 11.30 am, and said that the school children should be brought out of school and to church at that time. But on the first day of this new arrangement, at 11.30, the rector found that no children came to church. So then he made the decision to change the opening hours of the school. He put up a notice at school declaring that in future, the school would be opened between 9.00 am and 9.45 am for religious instruction – and children whose parents didn't want them to receive this instruction couldn't be admitted until 9.45 am. This put him in direct conflict with the school board.

After announcing this change in procedure, Reverend Hippisley duly arrived at school the next day at 9.00 am to teach the children religious instruction. At first, the master of the school board, Mr Teague, refused to let him in. Robert called for the police, but they refused to get involved. Eventually, he had to leave, but when he did, he was greeted by a group of locals, who laughed derisively at him. Robert announced that he would come again tomorrow. He then turned to the police sergeant and complained about his inaction, saying he would report it. At that, the crowd started laughing again. The rector, by now riled, asked what the meaning of their 'absurd laugh' was – but only made them laugh more.

The next day, Reverend Hippisley arrived again at school at 9.00 am, and attempted to teach a class, overriding the poor teacher. But Mr Teague was present, and told the children not to take any notice of the rector, as he was an intruder. The rector protested that the school wouldn't open till 9.45, 'in accordance with the provisions of the timetable'. But another member of the school board, Mr George Howman, said the timetable had been drawn up by Robert's instructions, and had never been submitted to the Board. Mr Teague then added that Robert had assumed a position which didn't belong to him, and that the board wouldn't allow him to domineer.

Whilst the power play was going on between the rector and the school board, the teachers were unable to teach, as Robert immediately countermanded every order given by the board members.

The problem was that Robert Hippisley wanted the school to be run as a Church of England school, but wanted ratepayers to pay for its running. As not all ratepayers were of the Church of England, the school board felt this was unfair. They had had a break from their troublesome vicar, as he had been on holiday for a fortnight, and had enjoyed the peace that had ensued in the town during his absence. Mr Teague wished he had stayed away, saying, 'You were not back in the town three hours before you began wrangling again. But we'll have no Czar of Russia here. Your autocratic rule is over – it is out of date.' Robert soon gave up, and left the school.

But he had not given up completely. The next day, he arrived again, with his new churchwarden, the young graduate Henry Wilkins, as his support. Wilkins attempted to do the 9.00 am

*Well Lane, Stow. The National School was opened here.* The author

prayers, but was grabbed by the board members and 'unceremoniously bundled' across the room and flung down the stairs. Wilkins was also seen as a troublemaker – at a vestry meeting the same week, there was a row between Wilkins and a Mr Blizard, when the latter called Wilkins 'a little bit of a boy' and Wilkins called Blizard a liar. It ended with Blizard hitting the churchwarden. At a vestry meeting in 1887, a petty argument over a minute book between Robert and his former churchwarden, Mr Turner, ended in a struggle and the rector falling over and breaking a chair.

Robert Hippisley's antics received a fair bit of coverage in the regional news – after all, it was not often that a vicar was so unpopular that his parish revolted in so blunt a fashion. The newspapers laughed at his eccentricities and failures – for example, when he failed to turn up to a wedding he was supposed to officiate at, and had to be woken up by the fire bell being rung. And locals wrote to the press about their vicar too; in February 1888, an E W Blackwell of Stow wrote to the *Cheltenham Free Press* claiming that the rector was a hypocrite, and had only been elected as chairman of the school board due to the 'inertion or ineptitude of the ratepayers'. He was also viewed by his parish as a power-hungry figure; Blackwell said, 'He would be glad to secure the economy if it could be done without relinquishing his cherished power', and when Hippisley complained of being ignored with regard to some land of which he was a trustee, a Mr Davis quipped, 'I wonder at you allowing yourself to be ignored!'

Another dispute came in 1887 with the occasion of the Queen's Golden Jubilee. Apparently, Hippisley had first said, 'there should be no unseemly merrymaking on that day', which riled his party-loving parishioners; and then he had proposed commemorating the jubilee by establishing a recreation ground. That was fine – but Hippisley wanted the local board to pay for it, boasting that he was the 'largest ratepayer in the local board district, and I am willing to do them good if they would let me'. A letter from 'Senex' in the local paper commented, 'That the rector does know best is a point which ... older inhabitants of Stow consider at least open to argument.'

Poems were also composed mocking the rector's actions. The school situation prompted the following lines: 'O, stormy Stow! Where tempers glow/And manners grow/Still less and less ...' And after Hippisley's row with Turner, a poem by 'Diogenes' appeared in the *Cheltenham Free Press* entitled *Turnerius (A Lay Of Ancient Stow)* that asked in vain for the people of Stow to stop arguing. It sums up the acrimony that often occurred at meetings chaired by the rector, implying that they were often characterized by 'noise and din'.

Although Hippisley won the argument with Turner, 'Diogenes' sees the latter as the true victor – 'it was no disgrace/ He fought bravely for his fellows/And for his native place.' The implication is that Turner, as a Stow-born local, has more integrity than the Berkshire-born Hippisley. But his propensity for instigating heated rows in church meetings proves the comment made about him in 1887 by Henry Wilkins – 'He is a gentleman of the old school, and fears not to call a spade a spade.'

One incident in particular reflects how Robert Hippisley was seen at least as a controversial figure by sections of Stow society. On Bonfire Night, the town usually celebrated by lighting a large bonfire on the town green, near the *Bell Inn*. On 5 November 1898, the traditional celebration was held. The bonfire only lasted a short time, and the youngsters who had watched it left for home.

But at 10.00 pm, many locals were awoken by a handbell being loudly rung in the street. Such a noise was not common at this time of night, and unsurprisingly, many people got up and went out to see what the noise was about. Very soon, a crowd had collected on Church Street. They saw a procession of people carrying an effigy at shoulder height. At first, it was thought the effigy was of a woman as it was dressed in a long black dress and black straw hat – but the attire was supposed to resemble a minister's somber clothing, and the effigy was, in fact, of rector Robert Hippisley.

The effigy was carried along Church Street and round Market Square into what was known locally as Hilly Park. The procession – its ranks swelled by the interesting bystanders – came to a halt in a field at the back of the rectory. Presumably witnessed by the horrified residents of the rectory, the effigy was then burnt. The crowd who witnessed this largely consisted of men and boys – together with the police sergeant, Sergeant Simpson, and several local constables (apparently there to ensure that no breach of the peace offence was committed; but they must have been spellbound by the sight of an effigy of one of the town's most prominent citizens being destroyed in sight of his own home). But the crowd was well-behaved, and after the effigy had burnt, they meekly dispersed and returned home to tell their families what they had just witnessed.

Apparently, Robert's reaction was to expel two young choristers from the St Edward's Choir, who, he believed, had been involved in the 'guying'. He had tried to get them to apologize for their actions, but they had refused. But Robert's actions angered the local youth even further, and the rest of the choir promptly went on strike until the two expelled choristers were re-admitted.

It cannot have been a coincidence that less than a week after the effigy of him was burnt, Robert announced his retirement from the rectorship of Stow. But this action did not mean that he had been humbled; he had received a glowing response to his resignation letter from the Archbishop of Cirencester, HR Hayward, and so sent it on to the *Oxford Journal*, asking for it to be published as 'it will interest your numerous readers'. Robert was, though, not just trying to publicize the Archbishop's view of the 'pleasant relations' he had enjoyed with him; he was also stressing the Archbishop's view that Robert should enjoy the 'peace and rest to which your years so well entitle you'. Robert may have believed that someone of his age and rank deserved gentle treatment and respect from those younger than himself, and felt offended that he had not been given this from many people in Stow.

By now a widower, and frail, Robert moved in with his unmarried daughter Gertrude, who lived at Beechwood House, off the Lower Swell Road in Stow. 1900 was a bad year for him, as he became increasingly feeble. On 14 January 1901, he slipped and fell whilst moving from the lavatory to another room in Beechwood House, and injured his thigh. He was already suffering from pneumonia, and his fall meant he was confined to bed, and was much weakened. Eventually, on 28 January, with his son William and daughters Grace, Alice, Gertrude and Eva present, Robert Hippisley died aged eighty-three.

His obituary in the *Oxford Journal* of 2 February 1901 recorded his achievements in somewhat guarded terms, noting:

*His long incumbency was marked by much unrest in the parish, his eccentricity leading him into frequent conflict with his colleagues and the local authorities.*

So the rector of Stow was remembered not so much as he had wanted, for his munificence and his monitoring of the local school system, but for the strife he had caused in the town over the previous sixty-odd years!

CHAPTER 16

# Satan Tempted Her:
# The Campden Poisoner

# 1835

The Cotswolds may have been full of drunken men committing foul deeds in the past, but not all crimes were drink-fuelled, and not all were committed by men. One particular crime, which occurred in Chipping Campden in 1835, attracted a lot of attention precisely because the criminal did not meet the normal stereotypes.

Harriet Tarver, née Tracey, was a twenty-one-year-old from the town, a young mother with a good record. She was from a local family – her parents, William, an agricultural labourer, and Sarah, were both from Chipping Campden and lived on Sheep Street in the town. She had married young, aged nineteen, to twenty-four-year-old local man Thomas Tarver. She must have struck Thomas, with her black hair, dark grey eyes and dark complexion. She had received some schooling, as she could read – but her reading was not perfect, and she had not learned to write. She helped her husband, who was a carrier, by working as a labourer. In September 1834, the couple had their first and only child – a daughter named Ann, after her paternal grandmother.

The young Tarver couple, and their baby, lived a normal working-class life in Chipping Campden for a year or so, attracting little attention. But then, on 11 December 1835, Thomas Tarver suddenly died after a very short illness. He was young and had previously been healthy, and so it was not surprising, especially in a small market town where everybody knew everybody else, that rumours that Thomas had been

*St James's Church, Chipping Campden, where Harriet Tracey and Thomas Tarver married.* The author

murdered soon started to circulate. An inquest was started on 15 December, but the jury was not presented with any concrete evidence of foul play, and so they requested that the inquest be adjourned until a week later. When the inquest resumed, the evidence the jury needed presented itself.

Arsenic had been found in Thomas Tarver's stomach. Several witnesses then came forward to say that Harriet Tarver had been seen buying two parcels of arsenic for no apparent reason. No one could think of any reason why she should want her husband dead, but then, no one could think of any other reason why she would buy the arsenic. The inquest jury returned a verdict of wilful murder against Harriet after a long deliberation, and she was duly committed for trial.

The trial was on Friday, 8 April 1836 at Gloucester, and Thomas Tarver's last day on earth was detailed. On Friday, 11

December 1835, he had gone to work early, at around 4.00 am – he worked at the *Noel Arms* in Chipping Campden. Only ten minutes after arriving at work, he became sick, complaining of a 'great heat' in his stomach. He was sick several times. By 2.00 pm, he was dead.

Two days before Thomas's death, Harriet had bought some rice pudding, and gave him some for his breakfast the day he died. The same day, Mr Holland – presumably some kind of doctor or quack – had given Thomas two pills for an unknown ailment. They were found to contain scorched wood-laurel, nitre, and flour, which wouldn't have done him any good, but neither would they have killed him. He had taken the pills on Wednesday, but on Thursday was quite well.

Harriet Tarver's behaviour was suspect immediately. Just a week before Thomas's death, she had been seen buying arsenic at a local shop. Her belief that she could buy poison in a Campden shop, where everyone knew her, and kill her husband with it only a week later, showed either supreme confidence or plain stupidity. And after his death, she had apparently said to people that she hoped to God nothing would be found in her husband's body when it was opened up.

But Thomas was opened, in a post-mortem carried out by surgeon Mr Hiron. He took out the stomach and its contents and sent them to a Dr Thomson in Stratford-upon-Avon, who was experienced in carrying out experiments to ascertain the presence of poisons. Dr Thomson said that he had never seen a stomach in the state Thomas's was in as a result of natural causes, so he was immediately suspicious. Dr Thomson carried out elaborate experiments involving copper and silver sulphates, and they resulted in positive results for the presence of arsenic. He said that from the stomach and stomach fluids, he obtained the equivalent of twenty-seven or twenty-eight grains of arsenic. In addition, Dr Thomson added, Thomas's vomiting would have thrown up a lot of the arsenic that he had originally been given, so the remaining grains would be just a small proportion of what he had taken. Thirty grains of arsenic would have been enough to have killed him. Dr Thomson scotched the idea that the pills Thomas had taken could have killed him. He said that he had never seen a case where scorched wood-laurel leaves were ingested, that they could be an acrid poison, but would have shown an effect within ten to twelve hours at the latest – and Thomas had been fine at that time.

On the basis of Dr Thomson's findings, and the evidence of the witnesses who had seen young Harriet buying arsenic, the jury, after an hour's deliberations, found Harriet Tarver guilty of murder. She had apparently been hopeful of an acquittal, and was shocked by the guilty verdict.

On her arrival at Gloucester Gaol, after the death sentence had been pronounced, Harriet confessed to killing Thomas. She said she had bought the rice pudding that killed her husband, with both her and her child eating some before she mixed the remainder with arsenic and put it in her kitchen cupboard, knowing her husband would take it and eat it later. She said, the local press later reported, that her motive for killing her young husband was that she was in love with another man, and saw killing him as a means for her to be able to be with this other man.

After her trial, Harriet spent the night in a cell at Gloucester Gaol trying to compose herself. Her lack of education meant that she had killed Thomas without thinking through the effects of her action properly. She had acted as a result of a passion for another man, and had never thought that she might be hanged as a result of this passion. She was young and naïve. Another woman, Ann Sherrington, who had just been acquitted of murder on the grounds of temporary insanity, was seen as a model woman for Harriet to copy. Ann, who had been charged with the wilful murder of her three-month-old son back in January, was seen as appropriately grateful for her acquittal, and penitent – and so she was allowed to stay in Harriet's cell with her, helping her to pray to God for forgiveness for her crime.

But Harriet was not given much chance to sit and reflect on what she had done. The day after her trial, on Saturday, 9 April 1836, just before 12.00 pm, she became the youngest woman in nineteenth century Gloucester to be hanged. There were an immense number of spectators, many of them women, waiting to see her executed. Although she was seen by the spectators to have shown great fortitude as she stepped up to the platform to have the noose put round her, she was not rewarded with a quick death; she moved her head, the noose slipped, and she took some time to die.

But after her death, she enjoyed some notoriety. Broadsheet ballads had been popular since the sixteenth century, and were cheap forms of entertainment, sold in the streets by itinerant sellers. They were verses about current events, both political and social, and one of the most popular forms was the broadsheet ballad featuring a notorious murderer. Today, people will read the salacious headlines in the tabloids with eagerness; in Harriet Tarver's day, the broadsheet ballad would provide the same entertainment. And just as with some of the more outlandish stories in the press today, the ballad might contain a substantial element of fiction. Although many ballads purported to have been written by the criminal, and be from their point of view, in reality, they were written by someone else and follow a standard format that included an ending whereby the criminal would be about to meet his or her maker, and often a warning for others not to follow their example.

Broadsheet ballads about murderers were often printed in advance to be sold at their execution. As executions often drew large crowds, all looking for a bit of entertainment, the ballads could sell well. A Cheltenham printer, Willey, sought to profit from Harriet's execution, and produced a single sheet entitled *An Affecting Copy Of Verses Written On The Body Of Harriet Tarver*. The presentation of the sheet, with its sub-heading setting out the date of the execution, makes it look like a souvenir of the event, like buying a programme at a football match. The ballad was illustrated with what obviously purported to be a likeness of Harriet herself; but the lady pictured looks some years older than Harriet, who was only twenty-one when she died, so was probably a 'standard' engraving put in the ballad in the absence of a likeness of Harriet herself.

The verses written about Harriet follow the standard format, setting out her name and her wicked deed. It describes Satan as having tempted her to kill her loving husband, and

# An Affecting Copy of Verses

Written on the Body of

# HARRIET TARVER,

Who was Executed April 9th, 1836, at Gloucester, for Poisoning her Husband in the town of Camden.

GOOD people all I pray attend.
Unto these lines that I have penn'd ;
A criminai confined I lie,
My crime is of the blackest die.

Harriet Tarver is my name, you'll hear,
From Camden town in Gloucestershire,
I own the dreadful deed I've done,
And now my glass is nearly run.

A loving husband once I had.
Which ought t, have made a wife's heart glad,
But Satan he tempted him so,
That I resolves the deed to do

To poison him was my intent,
And to take his life I was fully bent,
White arsenic I did apply,
Which for the same I'm condemned to die,

By him a lovely child I bore,
And alas I ne'er shall see it more.
O Lord thou be a parent kind,
To my orphan child which I leave behind ;

God grant it may a warning take,
Of its mother's untimely fate,
From the paths of vice and bad company
From all such crimes pray keep it free.

When my trial came on, you hear,
With a heavy heart I did appear,
The jury they did guilty cry,
And soon I was condemned to die,

Back to the death cell I was ta'en,
Forty-eight hours to remain,
And there my time to spend in prayer,
Hoping to meet my Saviour there.

You married women wheree'er you be,
I pray toke warning now by me,
Pray love your husbands and children to,
And God his blessing will bestow.

Hark ! now I hear my passing bell,
Now I must bid this world farewell,
And when the fatal bolt shall fall,
The Lord have mercy on my soul.

Willey, Printer, Cheltenham.

*The verses published to 'celebrate' Harriet Tarver's execution.* Cambridge University Library (ref Madden 23/403) emphasizes the fact that she was a mother, mentioning the 'lovely child' that she will no longer be able to see.

The writer then warns Ann Tarver to take a warning from her mother's 'untimely fate' and avoid vice and bad company. The ballad then gives a warning to married women to follow the conventional route to happiness – to love their husbands and children in order to gain God's blessing. Contemporary writers obviously saw Harriet as disobeying the rules of nature in failing to be a good wife or mother. But it is doubtful whether Harriet would have written in such emotional terms about Ann, for she had thought little of her one-year-old child when she bought the arsenic in Chipping Campden on that Wednesday in 1835.

# Chapter 17

# 'A Desperate Act': Infanticide in Dowdeswell

## 1817

If you were a poor woman in the nineteenth century Cotswolds, without a partner to support you, and you had a baby, how would you look after it? This was a question that faced a surprisingly large number of women in the area. Sex outside of marriage happened, and was not universally frowned upon, even well into Queen Victoria's reign. Prudish attitudes towards sex were evident, of course, but were more obvious amongst the educated classes, the media and London society. Rural society operated under its own rules and acts. Illegitimate children were born, and were often brought up by their mothers – and vicars were often surprisingly willing to baptize these 'base-born' children, and to give them a good, Christian, start to life.

But some mothers were unable to face the shame or the burden of bringing up a child without that child's father being around. They might, of course, be sexually naïve and panic when they gave birth; or they might just want to pretend that nothing had happened and carry on with their lives. In such cases, they might resort to drastic measures. Infanticide – the murder of one's child – was not an unusual crime in the Cotswolds; local newspapers and prison records abound with tales of mothers murdering their babies. It was a crime that aroused the ire and disgust of the local press and commentators.

But it was a crime that could solve the economic and personal problems that could face a woman who had an illegitimate child. And sometimes, women could successfully conceal their pregnancies and literally get away with murder.

In 1816, the bodies of two infants had been discovered between the joists of the floor in an unoccupied attic in the house of John Chandler at Aston on Carrant, just east of Tewkesbury. Both had been there for several years; one had been strangled – having still a handkerchief tightly wound round its neck – and the other had no obvious signs of injury so had perhaps been stillborn (its death would have been a crime, though, later in the century as the mother could have been charged with concealing a birth). The parents of these children were never traced.

But for every infanticide that went unnoticed, and for every mother who succeeded in killing her child and got away with the crime, there was another more unfortunate soul. Between 1735 and 1794, four women were executed in Gloucester for murdering their babies, and more were to come in the following century. Ann Tigh was one of them.

Ann was born around 1780 in Dowdeswell, near Andoversford, only four miles south-east of Cheltenham, but deep in the Cotswold countryside. The parish of Dowdeswell was small, having at that time fewer than 200 inhabitants, but it included several large estates and houses. Sandywell House was owned by Henry Brett in the early eighteenth century; he had created a large deer park that in 1770 had been re-landscaped in a contemporary style. Upper Dowdeswell Manor was in another part of the parish, and this also had a deer park, as did Upper House, later known as Dowdeswell Court, just below Lower Dowdeswell village. The rural area was affluent and life was enjoyed by its house and estate owners, but those living further down the social ladder did not enjoy such a good life.

Ann was a working woman, a labourer in the area. She was described as a widow, but I can find no record of her marriage in the Dowdeswell parish. She may, of course, have originally been from a different area and married in her home parish; but society at this time was far less mobile than we are today, and villagers didn't tend to move very far. There is also no record of the death of a Mr Tigh in Dowdeswell. In addition, when Ann's child was baptized, no father's details were recorded, hinting that perhaps there wasn't a Mr Tigh. If there had been, it was likely that his name would have been recorded in the baptism register, followed by 'deceased' in brackets.

Ann Tigh was a small woman, five feet one, with dark grey eyes and dark brown hair, a wide mouth and round face. Although working as a labourer, she was able to read a little. Perhaps she had been taught to read at Sunday school, in order that she would be able to read her Bible. There had been no need to teach her to write, as she was a working class girl and unlikely to need this skill.

Whatever Ann's status, in the summer or autumn of 1817, she must have realized that she was pregnant. She was in her late thirties by this point; although times were different, how naive was she? Was this her first experience of sex and its aftermath, or was she simply careless? Dowdeswell was not large, and her friends and neighbours must have worked out that she was expecting a baby. This probably would have been accepted by most of them as just something that happened, and not something to disown her for.

In the December of 1817, Ann gave birth to a little girl. Here, the facts are vague. On 15 December, little Phoebe Tigh was baptized at Dowdeswell parish church by the local rector, Reverend Barber, suggesting that she was still alive at this point. But on 19 December, Rev Barber was having to bury Phoebe. Her age was listed on the burial record as 'a few hours' old; so was she baptized hurriedly, very shortly before she died? Had Ann baptized her newborn daughter, then murdered her? Or had the authorities found the body of the hours old child, named her, and baptized her to help her way to Heaven – and then buried her after the circumstances surrounding her death had been established? The records don't answer these questions.

Eight days after Phoebe's burial, though, her mother was charged with her murder, following an inquest on the baby's body carried out by the local coroner, John Cooke. She was tried at the Lent Assizes on April Fool's Day 1818, and condemned to death. She should have been executed within a few days, but her sentence was delayed until the following month. This may have been because of her poor mental and physical state. She was reported to be an unhappy woman,

*Baptism entry for baby Phoebe Tigh at Dowdeswell.* © *Gloucestershire Archives* (ref P117/IN1/4)

who was completely lacking in mental firmness after she had been condemned. The local press believed that the realization of her impending fate had deprived her of her mental faculties, and also made her physically ill – unsurprising given the nature of her sentence. However, no one could make her acknowledge that her fate was fair.

It has to be remembered that these were the days before post-natal depression or puerperal psychosis had been diagnosed or recognized as fairly common side-effects of giving birth. Puerperal psychosis usually occurs, if it occurs at all, within the first month of the baby's life, leading the mother to become confused or delusional, and, in severe cases, causing them to harm their children. Ann's poor mental state may have been occasioned by the birth of Phoebe, and being the reason for the little girl being murdered. In the later nineteenth century, puerperal psychosis was used successfully as a defence in infanticide cases, with mothers often sent to asylums to have their illness 'corrected'. But in the early years of the century, there was no such defence, and infanticide trials were more black and white. The only hope for women charged with infanticide in the early nineteenth century was if the prosecution could not prove that they killed their child, only that they had tried to conceal the birth. Often, women would attempt to show that their child had been stillborn, or had died of natural causes – and in these more scientifically primitive days, it was harder to prove a child had been murdered unless it was fairly obvious (there were many cases in the nineteenth century of babies having their throats cut, although in one case, even the mother of a child who had been dismembered, and who had admitted carrying out the dismemberment, was acquitted of infanticide). Before 1861, concealing a birth was not an offence, so if infanticide could not be proved, women could not be guilty of a lesser offence, and could walk away free.

On the morning of 4 May 1818, Ann Tigh performed the customary religious rituals at Gloucester Gaol, although with some difficulty. She was so weak that she had to be supported by at least one person, and sometimes two people, during her last journey from the cells to the scaffold. She was supported by these people until the moment she was hanged. But hanged she still was, in front of a huge crowd of curious spectators. The thought of death was enough punishment for Ann, it seems, given her physical and mental collapse, but it wasn't enough for the people of the area and time. They believed in an eye for an eye, and wanted Ann to be punished for the death of little Phoebe Tigh by dying herself. They got their wish, and poor Ann's motives in killing her child – surely itself a desperate act – died with her.

# CHAPTER 18

# 'Too Quick to Use Their Staffs': Death at Tetbury Mop

## 1843

In some respects, the nineteenth century Cotswolds seem to have been a lawless region, an anglicized version of American Gold Rush towns, where shoot-outs would occur frequently, where trivial comments and arguments could easily turn into fatal incidents. Yes, there were men whose job was to maintain law and order, but either the locals weren't scared or intimidated by these people, or the lawmakers and officers were criminals themselves.

Not all men were lawbreakers, of course, but even those who were innocent men could easily find themselves caught up in trouble. The time of the annual Mop fair, a feature of most of the Cotswold towns in the nineteenth century, with some still existing today, was a time when people were particularly prone to get involved in trouble. The fairs were supposed to be a time when people who worked in service sought new employers; but they were becoming more of a social event; a time when people would eat, drink and be merry. These revelries had a darker side, with crimes, assaults and drunken behaviour being sadly common.

Llewellyn Alley was one man who became caught up in the problems associated with the Mops. He was born at Wotton under Edge around 1808, the son of Richard and Mary Alley. He married Alice Harris in Tetbury on 13 August 1832, and they settled in the town, where they had five children – Fanny, Henry, Mary Ann, Lewin Thomas and Frederick.

*Combers Mead, Tetbury, home of the Alley family.* The author

In October 1843, they were living a quiet life in Combers Mead, Tetbury, and Alice was pregnant with her sixth child. It also happened to be the time of the annual Tetbury Mop, and many of the town's residents were out and about in town.

Alice Alley chose to stay at home with their young children, who were then aged between three and eight, on the evening of the Mop. However, Llewellyn was out; either at the Mop, or at work. He was on his way home, and almost at his door, when he heard a woman calling for help, and for the police. Llewellyn reached his house, got Alice, and the two of them raced to find the woman. She was nearby, accusing a man of robbing her. Llewellyn grabbed the man by the collar, and asked Alice to go to the police station for help.

Alice did as she was told, and on telling the police what was happening, two plain clothes policemen, William Jones and James Bick, ran towards the spot where Llewellyn, who was, apparently, hatless (not the done thing in Victorian society) stood. Both the officers were fairly tall men, Jones being nearly 5' 9" and Bick 5' 7". Neither police officer told Llewellyn who they were, and as they were not in uniform, they might have looked just like any other onlooker, Jones with his sandy hair and whiskers, and Bick dark skinned with brown hair and eyes.

There were differing reports of what happened next. All agreed that Llewellyn was struck on the head several times by one of the policemen, using a constable's staff. Some said that the other man then struck him with a smaller stick, so hard that it broke. The policemen later stated that Llewellyn had struck one of them or that a stone had been thrown. James Bick said that William Jones had struck Llewellyn only once, and that he, Bick, had not struck him at all. They both sought to make Llewellyn look both aggressive and guilty, whilst making out that they had barely reacted. This was not the case.

Llewellyn Alley was so seriously injured from what was, according to James Bick, just one blow, that he had to be carried to the police station. Two surgeons attended him, and they tried everything they could think of to save him, but he died the following day.

It should be remembered that at this time, many police officers were men who took on the role in addition to a full-time job. James Bick, for example, was a young man, aged twenty-four, from the parish of Aston Ingham in Herefordshire. He was a labourer in addition to being a constable. William Jones, who was the same age as Bick, was from Upleadon in Gloucestershire, and worked as a shoemaker as well as being a PC. They were both from the same working-class stock as the men they were supposed to keep an eye on, and frictions must have arisen from this conflict between being one of the workers, yet also being part of the law-making community. In the first half of the century, at least, policemen were rarely respected or feared precisely because they came from the same class as many of the people they arrested.

They were certainly not above the law, either – or so it originally seemed. James Bick and William Jones were charged on the coroner's warrant with manslaughter. The coroner, Mr J G Ball, had considered a charge of murder, but the coroner's jury only took thirty minutes to dismiss this and unanimously return the lesser verdict. The jury might have had more respect

*Prison entry for James Bick and William Jones.* Gloucestershire Archives (ref Q/Gc5/7)

for policemen than the general community, and not believed that officers could be guilty of murder; or the facts were too confused to admit to the more serious charge.

Jones and Bick were charged on the Coroner's Inquisition on 8 October 1843 with feloniously killing and slaying Llewellyn Alley at Tetbury. They were committed to trial by the coroner, and were due to be tried at the Winter Assizes. On 4 November, though, James Bick was given bail and allowed to leave gaol; William Jones was not so lucky, or hadn't got friends or family with the money to put up bail, and remained in custody.

The pair were tried on 13 December 1843, but it was found that there was not a true bill against them, astonishingly, given the evidence against them. How a charge of manslaughter could not be brought against them is a mystery, although their status as policemen may have had influence. William Jones was discharged on 14 December; Bick, of course, was already free. They would receive no punishment for the injuries inflicted by Llewellyn Alley.

Alice Alley gave birth to Llewellyn's posthumous son in the spring of 1844. He was named Llewellyn in memory of his late father. Alice now had the difficult task of raising her large family on her own, and it proved a struggle. Seven years after her husband's death, she was listed as a pauper in the 1851 census. This was the same year that her daughter Mary Ann died, aged just thirteen. Alice had to work to look after her surviving children, and in subsequent censuses, her employment was given as 'laundress'. This was often a poorly paid job, but it was one that could be done from home, and Alice probably did it from her rented home in Cutwell Lane, Tetbury. From at least 1851 to 1871, she also had a long-term lodger – Charles Hughes, fourteen years her senior. She died, aged sixty-six, in 1874.

What happened to the two policemen who were rather too quick to use their staffs? James Bick, just twenty-four at the time of Llewellyn Alley's death, rose up the police ranks after Llewellyn's death. He got married two years later, and had two children. In 1851, he was a police sergeant based at Canonbury Street Police Station in Berkeley. By 1861 he was superintendent of police in Bristol. But by 1871, he had left the police, for unknown reasons, and was now living in Cheltenham and working as a carpenter. He died in 1880.

William Jones is harder to trace, Jones not being the most unusual name. However, it looks likely that he may have moved to London after the Llewellyn Alley trial, with his eldest child being born there in 1850. He then moved onto Swansea, and was living there by 1851. In that year, an Upleadon-born William Jones was living in Swansea with his wife and baby daughter, and working as a railway guard; between 1861 and 1881, he was a beer retailer or victualler in the town, and in 1901, this same Jones, now a ripe old eighty-three, was still in Swansea, widowed, and listed in the census as a retired licensed victualler. If this is the former constable, it shows that for whatever reason, he settled away from his home and family, and had to take on a variety of jobs to maintain his family. Unlike Bick, he did not make policing his main career.

# CHAPTER 19

# Unnecessary Interference: Murder After the Feast

## 1846

adly, Llewellyn Alley's death was not the only fatality at a Cotswold village event in the 1840s. Neither was it the only one where a policeman was involved. On 7 September 1846, a feast was held at Great Barrington, probably organized by George Talbot Rice, the third Baron Dynevor, for the villagers, many of whom probably worked for his estate at Barrington Park. Many of the 'peasantry', as the press patronizingly referred to the agricultural working class, were present. Such feasts were known for the tendency of the participants to get involved in arguments and violence, but this one had been different, a peaceful affair. Baron Dynevor's grounds were closed at some point in the early evening, and so the attendees moved on to find other sources of entertainment, mainly at local inns. Several men and women went to the *Fox Inn* in Windrush, and bought as much food and drink as they could afford. One group of agricultural labourers assembled in the inn's parlour: Reuben Busby, a man named Clifford (possibly William Clifford, aged around twenty-one), and two or three others. There were other assorted groups of people at the *Fox Inn*, but all were viewed as orderly and sober, although quite noisy at times.

The mood changed later in the evening, when a drunken man, apparently not part of Reuben's group, tried to join in, but then broke a glass. The inn's landlord tried to get him to pay for this damage, and he refused. The landlord then sent for the police. Sergeant Adams and two constables soon arrived, but one constable, James Probert, PC number 238, who was young and somewhat overeager, pushed an elderly man down on the floor. Probert was over five feet ten inches tall, and it probably didn't take much force to overpower the older man.

Clifford complained of the police's unnecessary interference, and the other men and women became exasperated at the police's presence. One of the constables left, but Probert drew his truncheon and, according to several witnesses, struck people randomly, swinging his truncheon both to left and right. This was despite no-one having committed a breach of the peace. Although Probert was the only policeman to wield his truncheon, it was noticed that his

*The* Fox Inn, *Windrush, where Reuben Busby met his death.* The author

sergeant remained at the inn's door, watching, and not interfering or trying to stop his constable. Probert hit Clifford repeatedly, until others dragged him out of the room to protect him. Probert then turned on poor Reuben Busby, who was sitting quietly at a table, and struck him with the truncheon on the crown of his head. He immediately fell to the floor, blood rushing from the wound, appearing lifeless. It took Reuben's injuries to bring the landlord, together with several other people, to stop Probert, and Reuben was taken outside to give him some air. He failed to regain consciousness, and the locals decided he needed medical help. A Burford surgeon, Mr Cheatle, was called for and came as soon as he could, but immediately saw that Reuben's case was hopeless. He administered stimulants, to no avail. Reuben was pronounced dead the next morning. His skull had been fractured so badly

*Great Barrington, home of Reuben Busby.* The author

that it was exposed, and brain matter had come out of the wound to his head.

Clifford, a native of Great Rissington, had also been injured, although reports varied as to how serious his injuries were. At one point he was thought to be gravely ill; but Mr Cheatle commented that although he had head and facial injuries, they were not, in fact, serious.

Probert, who was originally from Berkeley, and had previously worked as a blacksmith (he said he 'did not like that work'), surrendered himself to his sergeant before it was known that Busby had died, but such was the furore over his crime, that he had to be temporarily transferred to the custody of a constable in Great Barrington. The twenty-one-year-old was suspended from duty.

At Reuben's inquest, which was held at the *New Inn* in Northleach, Probert, through his solicitor, Mr Gaisford, tried to convince the jury that the police had been called in by the landlord of the *Fox Inn*, and therefore were acting in accordance with duty. Probert, according to this, was only using his truncheon in self-defence. The many witnesses – there were nearly thirty of them – were cross-examined by Probert's solicitor, but they were all firm in their belief that there had been no rioting at the inn, and that no resistance to the police had been shown that would justify the use of force. Mr Gaisford was so persistent in his cross-examinations that, at one point, the coroner had to remove him from the inquest room. Interestingly, the Calendar of Prisoners, in detailing Probert's previous employment record, says that he 'lived for three years with Mr Gainsford [sic]'.

The inquest was, as a result of the many witnesses who needed to be called, a long one, lasting five days and only finishing on Friday, 18 September. James Probert was also present at the inquest, as no one was sure what line of questioning would be taken, and therefore he might be needed to say something. Although he was not in custody at this point, he was apparently under close surveillance.

The coroner, John Barnett, gave the jury the choice of three verdicts – murder, manslaughter, and justifiable homicide. They took a long time to consider these choices. However, they came back with the centre course, manslaughter, and on 19 September, James Probert was formally committed for trial at the next assizes.

James Probert's trial, which was part of the Spring Assizes on 5 April 1847, was like a rerun of that four years earlier in Tetbury, when PCs Bick and Jones were tried for the murder of Llewellyn Alley. James was only charged with manslaughter, but there were, as the calendar of prisoners records, 'diverse witnesses' to give evidence that he had indeed killed poor Reuben Busby.

But despite the policeman only being charged with a more minor crime than murder, and despite all the evidence, the jury acquitted him. He was formally discharged on 9 April. Was it any surprise that the policeman, who had known the local solicitor defending him for several years, was acquitted? Despite his humble background as a blacksmith, Probert was regarded as part of the law-making society, and others didn't want to believe he could in fact be a lawbreaker.

Attention was being called to the behaviour of some sections of the nation's police, as a result of cases such as this and the previous one of Llewellyn Alley. The press argued that it had frequently had to draw attention to acts of violence by the police, and the consensus was that Reuben Busby was killed in an act of unprovoked brutality. People argued that the police had to be made an example of, to show policemen that they could not use their truncheons against innocent people, or use them unnecessarily when faced with trivial disputes. It seems obvious that rural policemen received little training in how to deal with certain situations, and so were prone to over-reacting.

Respect for the rural police was being eroded by these publicized examples of aggression on the part of policemen, and it seems the police responded to this by being overly sensitive to criticism by local people, further increasing the risk of them losing their tempers. The public's faith in their local police forces was being eroded, and the lack of accountability in these trials further antagonized them. But whilst young men with little experience were employed to protect them, the problems would continue.

# CHAPTER 20

# A Geographical Confusion: The Reprieve That Came Too Late

## 1811

Some criminals are cunning, some criminals are stupid, and some are just plain unlucky. Winchcombe's William Townley was one criminal who had just one too many instances of bad luck in his chequered career – one that led to his unnecessary death.

Winchcombe was, in the eighteenth century, a small town with a rich history, having the grand Sudeley Castle just outside the town. But its fortunes had been spoilt by the Dissolution in the 1530s, with Winchcombe Abbey being destroyed and nearby Hailes Abbey also acquiescing to Henry VIII, and even now, 250 years later, the town was not back to its former prosperity. In the late nineteenth century, it had been a small town largely populated by agricultural labourers, and one hundred years earlier, this had been equally the case.

William Townley was born in the town in 1781, being christened in St Peter's Church on 28 January. There were several Townleys in the town at the time, including a couple of Williams; the William Townley who was the son of William and Mary Townley seems to be the most likely candidate here. He had at least one sibling that we know of – brother John, three years his senior.

Although William's parents appear to have been an ordinary, law-abiding lot of people, William and John chose a different path. From their teens, they were committing crimes, and in 1799, when William was still just seventeen-years-old, the brothers were caught in an act of burglary. They were both

*Winchcombe, home of William Townley.* The author

convicted, and William was sent to the local Penitentiary House for two years.

In 1801, William was released, but he was soon offending again, and was charged with a capital offence in 1803. He was found guilty and ordered to be transported for seven years.

At this time, convicts were transported to Australia, the first party of convicts having been sent out to Botany Bay a quarter of a century before William's conviction. In the eighteenth century, stealing items over five shillings would have carried the death penalty, but times had become a bit more enlightened, and judges were viewing this punishment for petty theft as too severe – so transportation became more common, certainly for a first or second offence.

But William's punishment was even worse than it might seem. Instead of being sent to Australia, he was kept for seven years on one of the convict ships at Woolwich. The prison ships, known as 'hulks', were old warships that were moored on the Thames and intended to be a temporary holding bay, to house prisoners waiting to be transported. However, they

*View of the prison hulk* Justitia, *one time home of William Townley.* The National Maritime Museum, Greenwich, London (ref PZ9265)

proved in many cases to be a substitute for transportation. At the beginning of the nineteenth century, the three most infamous prison hulks were the *Prudentia*, the *Retribution* and the *Justitia*. William Townley was sent to the *Justitia*, a 260-ton, somewhat elderly ship, which had been used as a prison hulk since at least 1777. Goodness knows what state it was in by the time William got there, but the hulks were notoriously bad in terms of conditions and the number of prisoners kept on them.

Imagine the frustration of knowing you were on the river, surrounded by the delights of London and its suburbs, yet trapped on this stationary ship, in close confines with 400 others, sleeping in chains or fetters, in cramped cells barely high enough to stand in, with a lack of fresh food and air. The convicts were demeaned, had their clothes taken away from them, and were fed a monotonous diet. They were punished with floggings, or being placed in solitary confinement in tiny, dark cells. They had to work all day, being woken early in the morning. Occasionally, they emerged into the daylight, but only to work in a dingy grouping of workshops, warehouses and industrial premises known as the Woolwich Warren. William had seven years of this, before being discharged on 26 July 1810. His entry in the list of convicts on board the *Justitia* includes a laconic mention of his character: 'Townley, William ... Supposed to have committed many robberies.'

It is probably no surprise that such barbaric punishments failed to put an end to William's criminal career. By the nineteenth century, journalists and writers were wondering whether these punishments had any benefits, and expressing doubt as to whether men had any chance of being reformed as a result of their incarceration. William had been institutionalized, spending much of his late teens and early twenties incarcerated in one form or another. What sort of legitimate work could he expect to find on his release? With little money or education, the likelihood is that he would have to return to Winchcombe and get work as an agricultural labourer. But what farmer would choose to employ this young man with little work experience except that of stealing?

In all fairness, William did try and find other, legal, ways of obtaining money, and working. On his release from the prisoner ship at Woolwich, he signed up as a substitute in the Worcestershire Militia, for which he should have received forty guineas. He received the first ten, and promptly squandered it. Finding himself without money again, he then decided to

# For Lent Affizes, 1811.

1 *Joseph Thomas*, aged 35, committed September 13, 1810, by George Cooke, D. D. charged upon the oaths of Francis Evans and Mofes Higgs, upon fufpicion of having early this morning felonioufly ftolen, taken, and carried away, two ewe fheep, from and out of the parifh of Wapley and Codrington, the property of Elizabeth Williams. Alfo charged upon the oaths of John Wickham and William Godwin, with felonioufly taking, ftealing, and carrying away, early this morning, a quantity of hay, about twenty pounds in weight, of the value of 6d. the property of Henry Williams, of the parifh of Wapley and Codrington aforefaid.

2 *John Mealing*, aged 58, committed October 3, 1810, by John Hippifley, Clerk, charged on fufpicion of ftealing eleven ftore pigs, of the value of 11l. at the city of Gloucefter, on Friday laft, the property of William Pope, of Weftbury-upon-Severn.

3 *Francis Haves*, aged 50, } committed October 13, 1810, by James Commeline, Clerk, charged on the oath of
4 *Thomas Dandy*, aged 31, } Jofeph Maddocks, of Churcham, yeoman, on fufpicion of having, between the hours of one and two this morning, burglarioufly broken open the dwelling-houfe of him the faid Jofeph Maddocks, fituate at Churcham aforefaid.

5 *Robert Lane*, aged 33, committed October 16, 1810, by Richard Wetherell, Clerk, charged on the oaths of John Morgan, Thomas Hawkins, and Jofeph Stephens, on fufpicion of having ftolen one lamb, from and out of the parifh of Harefield, the property of the faid John Morgan.

6 *Thomas Adey*, aged 11, committed October 19, 1810, by Henry Burgh and Samuel Wathen, Efqrs. and William Mills, charged upon the oath of Richard Blackmore, with felonioufly breaking open the dwelling-houfe of him the faid Richard Blackmore, at the parifh of Horfley, on Tuefday laft, with an intent to commit a felony therein.

7 *William Townley*, aged 29, committed October 29, 1810, by Martin Lucas, Efq. charged on oath on fufpicion of ftealing, out of the houfe of George Skinner, a coat and two fhirts, of the value of 7s. the property of the faid George Skinner.

8 *Elizabeth Pearce*, aged 18, committed November 2, 1810, by Samuel Wathen, Efq. charged on the oaths of John Dubber and Hannah Franklin, with felonioufly picking the pocket of the faid John Dubber, on Monday evening laft, of about 130l.

9 *Jacob Cleavely*, aged 21, committed November 17, 1810, by Henry Anthony Pye, Clerk, charged on the oaths of William Price and Thomas Curtis, with fufpicion of having, in the night of Tuefday, the 13th of November inftant, felonioufly broken and entered the dwelling-houfe of the faid William Price, at Duntfborne Lear, and ftolen therefrom a fmock-frock, a filk handkerchief, a cotton handkerchief, and various other articles, his property.

10 *William Brewer*, aged 36, committed November 27, 1810, by Richard Branfby Cooper, Efq. charged upon the oaths of Robert Harris, alias Morton, and of Mary Morton, and others, on fufpicion of having unlawfully, wilfully, and felonioufly occafioned the death of Richard Gabb, a boy of eleven years of age, by beating him when in a weak and helplefs condition, and then leaving him in a ftate of infenfibility to perifh without affiftance, on Saturday evening, the 10th inftant, at Beverftone.

11 *James Hawkins*, alias *Parfley*, aged 25, committed December 14, 1810, by Charles Ludlow Walker, Efq. charged on the oath of Edward Parker, on fufpicion of felonioufly killing one fat fheep, value 40s. the property of him the faid Edward Parker.

12 *John Bowyer*, aged 19, committed December 16, 1810, by Richard Slade, Clerk, charged on the oath of William Vick, of Yate, yeoman, with felonioufly taking, ftealing, and driving away, in the night time between the 14th and 15th days of December inftant, two pigs, the property of the faid William Vick, of the value of 5l. 5s. from his fold or barton, in the faid parifh of Yate.

13 *Ann White*, aged 36, } committed December 21, 1810, by Henry Burgh and Henry Cooke, Efqrs. and William
14 *Jofeph White*, aged 14, } Mills, Clerk, charged on the oath of Philip Warhen, with felonioufly ftealing and carrying away, in the night of Tuefday, or the morning of Wednefday laft, one ewe fheep, from a field fituate in the parifh of Stroud, the property of the faid Philip Wathen.

15 *Daniel Prewett*, aged 37, committed January 4, 1811, by Humphry Crefwicke, Efq. charged on the oath of James Stone, on fufpicion of felonioufly ftealing a black gelding, value 5l. the property of him the faid James Stone.

16 *Sarah Leech*, aged 33, committed January 7, 1811, by William Joyner, Efq. Coroner, charged with the wilful murder of a new-born male baftard child.

17 *William Bennett*, aged 55, committed January 12, 1811, by Caleb Carrington, Clerk, charged on fufpicion of ftealing from a cheefe-loft in the houfe of William Riddiford, at Hill, cheefe of the value of 4l. the property of the faid William Riddiford.

*The list of cases being heard at the 1811 Lent Assizes included that of William Townley.* Gloucestershire Archives (ref Q/SG2)

commit another burglary to sort out his financial problems. He can't have been a very good burglar, though. In October 1810, he broke into the house of one George Skinner, and stole a coat and two shirts, worth a total of seven shillings, presumably to sell on later. He was promptly caught and committed to Gloucester Gaol on either 26 or 29 October (accounts differ), charged with burglary. The maximum penalty for stealing goods worth over five shillings was death.

At his trial in March 1811, several witnesses were called to give evidence against twenty-nine-year-old William. He brazenly declared that they had all sworn falsely against him. The jury decided otherwise, and sentenced him to death. He was due to be executed on Saturday 23 March – executions usually falling the Saturday after the verdict was given – and just before being given the sacrament, he admitted his guilt over the burglary.

But whilst William was preparing to meet his maker, wheels were being set in motion to give him another chance in life. The judge who had presided over William's trial had left Gloucester and was making his way to Hereford, the next town where assizes were held. Whilst on his way, he was notified of facts that were favourable towards William's case, and he made the decision to grant William a reprieve.

So far, so good. But now, a catastrophic mistake was made. The decision to reprieve William should have been passed on to the undersheriff of Gloucestershire. Instead, the letter containing the reprieve was directed to Mr Wilton or Woolaston, the Herefordshire undersheriff, and left at the Hereford post office. There it stayed until the letters were delivered – which wasn't until the next morning. If it had been addressed correctly, it would then have arrived safely in Gloucestershire, and William would have been home and dry. But instead, it turned up in Hereford. When it was opened by Mr Wilton and Mr Bird, the undersheriffs, they realised immediately its importance, they got a local hotel keeper, Mr Bennet, to get a fleet horse and ride with the letter to Gloucester, thirty-four miles away.

Poor Mr Bennet rode like the clappers, and reached Gloucester in good time – but William Townley had been executed just twenty minutes earlier, and was still hanging from the gallows.

Then, as now, the post office came in for a mauling by the press, with contemporary journalists astounded that the life of a man was not seen as important enough for a special messenger to be hired to get the reprieve to Gloucester – why was the letter just left for the postman to deliver? Thanks to the judge's geographical confusion, and the late delivery of one letter, William Townley never received the one piece of good luck that had come in his life.

# CHAPTER 21

# Unnecessary Suffering:
# Child Neglect and Poverty

## 1898

A short, sad story I came across whilst researching this book is included here at the end to show both how, even relatively recently, the dark side of the Cotswolds still existed – but also to show how things were slowly being altered and measures taken to protect the most vulnerable in society.

It can be seen from the case of Ann Tigh that many women could not cope with the idea of having an illegitimate child in the past, even if the attitude of neighbours was often surprisingly forgiving. The case of Clara Lambert, at the end of the nineteenth century, was an illustration of how, even if a woman kept her illegitimate child, it didn't mean she would learn to love it. If a new partner came onto the scene, the mother's feelings might be compromised, and financial worries could be increased by the presence of a child.

Ellen Augusta Lambert was a young woman from Ewen, a small hamlet near Cirencester. She was born in 1880, the second child of Henry, a groom, and his wife Ann. But sadness blighted her childhood; in 1885, Henry died, aged just twenty-eight, leaving his wife heavily pregnant and with three daughters aged between three and six to look after. Another daughter was born in the winter of 1885. The family moved from Ewen to nearby Somerford Keynes, and Ann started work as a charwoman to support her family. As her daughters got older, they found work as servants.

At the age of sixteen, Ellen Lambert became pregnant. She was unmarried and must have worried about giving birth to an illegitimate child. Her employment would finish as few people would want to employ an unmarried pregnant woman. But Ellen chose to have her baby, and in the first quarter of 1897, she gave birth to a little girl she named Clara.

At about the same time, in Rendcomb, another family was being left motherless. Mary Jane Curtis, aged thirty-three, was dying. Her husband, Elijah, was an agricultural labourer from Daglingworth. He was forty-eight, and had lived at home with his parents until he married Mary Jane Higgins, then a twenty-one-year-old servant, in 1884. The couple had four children together – Eli, Cornelius, Emily and William, who were, at this time, between six and twelve years old. Mary died early in 1896, leaving Elijah a widower, looking for someone to share the burden of looking after his young children.

At some point, Elijah and Ellen met; perhaps Ellen had known the Curtis family since before Mary's death. It is likely that Ellen had met Elijah working on a local farm, casual labouring being one of the job options open to a single mother. By the end of 1898, they were living in Hawling, near Guiting Power, and Elijah seems to have been working at Hawling Lodge Farm as they were allowed to live rent-free in one of the Hawling Lodge cottages.

A relationship between the two offered benefits for both; Elijah had a woman to help look after his sons and daughter, and Ellen gained a bit of respectability with a widower at her side and a home to live in.

Ellen Lambert and Elijah Curtis married in the winter of 1898, when Ellen was eighteen and Elijah was fifty. Ellen seems to have been pregnant at their wedding, as their daughter Beatrice was born around the same time as the marriage. Now Ellen was stepmother to four children under fourteen, and mother to two children only a year apart in age – and yet she was still in her teens. She had a lot of mouths to feed, and a lot of responsibility for someone so young. It is no wonder, perhaps, that something had to give.

There was not much money in the Curtis household. Elijah worked as a farm cowman, Eli as an under-carter and Cornelius as a stable-boy, probably all on the same farm – but their combined wages were only one pound a week. However, Elijah and Ellen had still managed to insure the life of Clara

*St Edward's Church, Hawling. Ellen and Elijah Curtis baptized their son James here just months after Clara Lambert's death.* The author

Lambert with the Prudential Insurance Company for seventeen pounds. Their cottage was fairly clean, and the Curtis children were well cared for.

But Clara Lambert seems to have been treated differently from the other children. Perhaps it was the stigma of her illegitimate birth and long gone father. Did Ellen resent her daughter, or did Elijah? Whatever the case, on 9 December 1898, Ellen Curtis wrote to Winchcombe doctor William Cox and asked him to come and look at Clara. Dr Cox visited, and found Clara lying on a heap of dirty clothes. Aged one year and eleven months, the little girl was emaciated, weighing less than one stone, her body covered in sores from head to foot. Her bed was rotten straw. Dr Cox believed that she must have been ill for quite a while, and promptly reported the case to the NSPCC, who investigated reports of child neglect. He then ordered that Clara be removed to the workhouse.

Clara could not get enough of the workhouse's meals, eating as though her life depended on it – which, in a way, it did. For about a week, she seemed to be improving, but then she started refusing food and around 14 December, she died of starvation.

The NSPCC prosecuted Ellen and Elijah Curtis under the Prevention of Cruelty Act 1894 for neglect and causing unnecessary suffering to Clara Lambert. They were also, initially, charged with manslaughter, but this charge was not proceeded with when they came to trial. Ellen and Elijah could not afford a defence team, and so Ellen submitted a written statement arguing that the Curtis men's wages were not enough to feed a family of eight, and denying that they had neglected Clara. She also said that Clara had been very weak since she was around four months old, and was barely able to move her arms and feet. Ellen added that she fed her daughter 'as much fat pork as she could eat, as well as other food, and what more could they do?'

The judge seems to have had sympathy for their plight; he believed that as they had asked the doctor to visit, they did not realize their treatment of Clara was wrong or that it would be criticized. He also refused to look at how or why they had insured their daughter's life (there is no mention of whether the other children were insured or not). It appears that the judge thought the couple's actions were taken due to a lack of education and money, and were, accordingly, understandable.

Ellen and Elijah Curtis were found guilty of neglect, with the judge holding them equally responsible, but the jury recommended them to mercy. For the sad life and tragically early death of Clara Lambert, her mother and stepfather each received three months' hard labour. After their release, they returned to their Hawling cottage, and had several more children together – one, James, being born the same year that they were imprisoned – before Elijah's death in 1917.

This story shows how many complex and sad stories there are to be found in the Cotswold records. Throughout history, poorer families have found themselves faced with tough choices, and both children and adults have suffered as a result. Some of these cases were publicized in the press; many, though, weren't deemed newsworthy enough. By the time of Clara Lambert, agencies such as the NSPCC were getting involved, and parliament was taking action. In 1889, the Children's Charter was passed. This was the first Act that aimed to protect children from cruelty, and it gave the police the powers to enter the home of any child thought to be at risk and to arrest anyone found mistreating a child. But by the time anything could be done, it was sometimes too late, and these measures didn't do anything to address the underlying issues of poverty, unemployment or lack of education. But times were, slowly, changing.

# Index